Jerri,

Can Change

your life,

magic

Jim

Hawk Rising

Soaring on the Wings of Desire

How to Manage Creative Anxiety

John Cowan

iUniverse, Inc.
New York Bloomington

Hawk Rising
Soaring on the Wings of Desire

Copyright © 2009 by John Cowan.

All rights reserved. No part of this book may be used or reproduced by any means, graphic, electronic, or mechanical, including photocopying, recording, taping or by any information storage retrieval system without the written permission of the publisher except in the case of brief quotations embodied in critical articles and reviews.

The views expressed in this work are solely those of the author and do not necessarily reflect the views of the publisher, and the publisher hereby disclaims any responsibility for them.

iUniverse books may be ordered through booksellers or by contacting:

iUniverse
1663 Liberty Drive
Bloomington, IN 47403
www.iuniverse.com
1-800-Authors (1-800-288-4677)

Because of the dynamic nature of the Internet, any Web addresses or links contained in this book may have changed since publication and may no longer be valid.

ISBN: 978-1-4401-4127-0 (sc)
ISBN: 978-1-4401-4128-7 (cloth)
ISBN: 978-1-4401-4129-4 (ebk)

Printed in the United States of America

iUniverse rev. date: 6/3/2009

Contents

Why Read This Book? 1
The First Parable: The Heart of a Tiger 3
Chapter One: Ruminations on a Flat Tire 5
Chapter Two: How You Became Anxious 17
Chapter Three: The Creative Anxiety Model 29
The Second Parable: The Disappearing Puppet 41
Chapter Four: Pictures 43
Chapter Five: Observing 57
Chapter Six: Anxiety 67
The Third Parable: The Motorcycle Club 77
Chapter Seven: Feeling-Response and Intention 79
Chapter Eight: Creative Anxiety 87
The Last Parable: The Hawk and the Fox 101
Summary of the Creative Anxiety Process 103
Several Exercises 105
My Bookshelf 109
About the Author 113

Why Read This Book?

Thousands and tens of thousands in the Western world have sought a brighter life through the practice of Eastern meditation. While many have experienced a deeper sense of calm, most have never experienced the enlightenment promised by these methods. Instead, practitioners become adept at sitting for long periods and observing their breath.

That was not what they had in mind when they began the practice. *Hawk Rising* will provide them a way of being that respects their present practice and will take them off the meditation mat and bring new brightness to everyday life.

On the other hand, thousands and tens of thousands have sought satisfaction by endlessly pursuing the ever-receding dreams of marketing culture. They have thought meditation practice anathema to their desires. And it is! However, here is a calming approach derived from the Buddhist system that will soften without stifling the desire for achievement to the point where good things are acquired as blissful experiences occur.

The Method:

Eastern meditation calls for awareness of the now, but it limits its definition of the now. It does not take into account the imagination other than to define it as "monkey mind," a nuisance to be at worst borne with, and at best, quieted. This method flows inevitably from the worldview of the Buddha and the East that the world is going nowhere and the creative imagination has little purpose.

But the western practitioner has been educated from birth and is being educated by his or her surroundings right now that the world is going somewhere. Flowing from this perspective, *Hawk Rising* views the imagination as part of the now and its work as something to be integrated into awareness.

The result of this integration is the end of frustration and the ability to step with power into everyday life. The imagination, which has been ignored until now, takes its rightful place of dominance at the same time as its shenanigans are brought to order and purpose through observation as learned in the *vipassana* tradition.

The Style:

The style of *Hawk Rising* is anecdotal, far ranging, casual, fun, witty, delightful, sometimes puzzling. It is designed to pull the reader along, induce experiences of brightness, and deposit him or her at the end of the trip with a gut-level understanding of a new way to sort and sift life.

The First Parable:
The Heart of a Tiger

Once upon a time, a tiger passed an ashram in India. The guru was a kind and loving teacher surrounded by one hundred kind and loving monks. Each day they rose before dawn and sat in lotus position in humble silence, being aware of their breath and their bodies and their feelings and their thoughts and that which surrounded them.

All of these silently seated people interested the tiger, so she asked the guru why they did what they did. "They are there to forget themselves and to learn what it means to be deeply human," responded the guru.

No one had ever suggested such a possibility to the tiger, and struck by it she noted that she had never done anything to learn what it meant to be a tiger, and certainly nothing to forget herself. She asked the guru what she could do.

"Join the ashram," he said, "eat no more of other animals, listen to talks about the meaning of life, sit for long periods being aware of your breath and your body and your feelings and your thoughts and that which surrounds you. Become a monk like us."

This seemed good to the tiger, so she began to do as suggested. She took a vow in front of the others to do as they did and search as they searched. Days went by, and then weeks. Carrots and radishes did not suit her. She grew thinner. Sitting weakened her once wire strong body. On the rare occasions that she moved, she found that her natural grace was deserting her.

In the middle of the second month, as she and all the monks were rising from sleep, with a leap and three bounds she covered the distance from the side of the clearing where she slept to the bed of the kind and loving guru. And she ate him. The other monks were horrified.

"What have you done?"

"I have discovered what it means to be deeply a tiger," she said as, licking her chops, she looked around for whatever other monk she might eat next. Noting her lean and hungry look, the monks began to shrink back, aware of her not so loving intentions.

Suddenly one of the monks grabbed a bamboo pole, bashed it against a rock to splinter its end, leaped to the center of the widening circle, and then drove the pole through the heart of the tiger. As the tiger lay dying and the monks turned to him in gratitude, he began collecting his bowl and mat to take his leave of the ashram.

"Why are you leaving just when you have saved our lives?" cried the eldest monk.

He replied, "Why should I stay? I have just forgotten myself and learned what it means to be deeply human."

Chapter One:
Ruminations on a Flat Tire

My Experiments with Meditation Practice

This starts earlier than the flat tire. Perhaps it starts twenty years ago when a friend suggested that I attend a five-day *vipassana* meditation retreat. At the time I was an Episcopal priest, so the invitation to a Buddhist event might seem unlikely. However, the friend who issued the invitation was a witch, and you can see how a priest who has a witch for a friend might do unlikely things. Before being an Episcopal priest, I was a Roman Catholic priest who from the seminary on religiously read Zen texts, so it was even likely that I would be invited to a *vipassana* retreat. And now I am a Quaker. After three major religious changes, stability should not be expected from me. The experimental is ordinary.

Whatever the likelihood, I did go to the retreat and began the daily practice of observing with loving attention the breath and whatever else came up.

I found this an invaluable addition to my spiritual life. At last I had something that I could do regularly that made a difference in my deepest understanding of the nature of life, and the nature of myself. At the same time, I was absorbed in scholarship about what Jesus really said and did in his brief stay on earth. These two sources of wisdom became meat and potatoes for my spirit.

To refresh the meditation practice, from time to time I attended other such long retreats. I had just finished checking in to one of them at the Franciscan retreat center we frequented in those days when Sister Ellen, a Franciscan nun with whom I had chatted on other occasions, asked me how long I was staying. (In deference to the needs of people, there was a choice of attending the weekend only or continuing for nine days of complete silence.)

I told her I was there for the longer period and started down the steps to the meditation room. As I walked away, I heard her say, "Oh, I did not think you were the type."

Since in the course of the next week almost nothing else was said to me directly, those last words kept recurring in my mind. *What the *#^* did she mean by "You're not the type?"* I had no idea.

First thing at the end of the silence, I sought her out and asked her. Her answer was: "You are too restless to last that long."

My retort was: "Well, I did last that long!" She nodded, but skeptically.

Suspicious Behavior

I had to admit there was reason for her doubt. About day three the leaders had begun complaining that some people were not following the spirit of the retreat. I suspected that they had noted my bicycle locked to a pole outside of their bedrooms (the only safe place I could find), and they had also noted that it disappeared every afternoon around three to return about five. I was not the only person cheating a little on their plan, but probably one of the more obvious. I found the two strenuous hours on the bicycle a marvelous relief from the physical inactivity of the other twenty-two hours. Like a soaring hawk, I found relaxation in the freedom of the roads after the confinement of the meditation room.

At one point on day three, one of the leaders said that the workshop had been carefully designed and those interfering with the schedule would lose all hope of great advances in their awareness. In my twelve years of seminary life (from freshman year of high school through four years of postgraduate study), I had been guilted often enough by past masters of the trade who wanted me to live within their boundaries that this attempt washed off without effort on my part.

Indeed, I nearly giggled as I imagined the leaders designing the workshop saying to each other:

"What should we do next?"

"Let's do sitting meditation!"

"Oh, what a good idea. That will work well since just before it we have walking meditation, and before that sitting meditation."

"You know, I bet people will be surprised and stunned if after this sitting meditation, we fed them a change and did walking meditation."

"Oh, Charlie, you are so brilliant. And then we could break for lunch."

"Smooth move, Lydia. They would never expect that at noon, especially if we call it eating meditation."

At one of those retreats, late October, it was frigid in the building. The meditation room and the cafeteria were comfortable, but everywhere else it was about sixty degrees. This would be fine if I were moving around with some vigor, but walking meditation does not get the blood running and sitting in my room gave me the chills. At night when the temperature dropped further, I piled on every blanket I could find. So I wrote a note to the managers (those assigned to keep the logistics working), complaining of the cold. The next morning one of them rose to say that there had been one complaint about the cold. Sixty-five people and one complaint. Me!

They went on to say that they had taken that complaint to the nuns, and the nuns had informed them that they do not turn on the heat for another week. Case settled!

I had been noticing this. While most of the teachers seemed vigorous enough, there was a definite tendency for students to begin to wimp out. Many of them when talking, for instance during question periods, sounded as if they had laryngitis. I had paid a lot of money to the nuns to stay in that place, and I thought they damn well should have turned on the heat. But I carried the argument no further. One against sixty-five was daunting, even for me, and I had come to meditate (and bicycle a little) but certainly not to engage in battle.

I once listened to a Zen abbot from the east coast speaking at the local *zendo* in St. Paul. He told of hiring a backhoe to do some excavating around the monastery. The job went on for an extensive time, so he and the operator in their many conferences about which rock was to go where became quite friendly. The abbot found the operator quite a Zen-like guy, with a great sense of the appropriateness of placement and respect for the nature of the phenomena he was pushing from here to there. After a month, possibly emboldened by their previous exchanges, the operator asked the abbot why it was that all of the monks walked around slowly with folded hands and downcast eyes, as if they were sneaking through life.

The abbot answered, "I have no idea! I never told them to do that."

This is not typical of everybody who engages in meditation. I have a *sensei* for a personal friend, and challenging his manhood might get me hurt. At the same time, there appears to me to be something suspicious going on here—a sapping of the vigor required for life. My friend the witch gave up her practice for a while because it was interfering with the flow of blood in her body. (Don't ask me how one feels the flow of blood. I accept much that I do not understand.) I know others who felt they could not do this meditation and succeed at their jobs, so they dropped the practice in favor of more vigorous pursuits.

What Is Up?

As the kids say: "Whazzup?" Not enough to stop my meditating or my living. I even wrote a book on meditation of which I am quite proud; and on the living side, I ride ten thousand miles on a midsize motorcycle every summer, camping half the nights. Meditation has not shut off the flow of my blood. Still and all, I do ask, "Whazzup?"

Why should this practice bring deadness when its purported author, the Buddha himself, said that he was waking up? How can waking up create sleepy people?

As a young man, I was interested in the stories of the Zen monks and hermits of the early days, wandering the hills searching for enlightenment. A friend of mine refers to them as "the Zen crazies." These are the guys who, when asked the meaning of life, belched. Died upside down in a corner to prove they could. When asked where to find Bosho, waved the questioner down the road, although the person asked was Bosho. Just a Bosho who had deliberately forgotten he was Bosho and did not want to be reminded.

What did these nuts have to do with sixty people sitting solemnly in a room observing the breath? As a matter of fact, the sixty were often the butt of the joke. The student rises from the crowd, goes to the teacher's platform, bows solemnly, knocks the teacher off the platform, and seats himself on the teacher's pillow. The teacher rises, dusts himself off, bows to the student, and then hammers him off the pillow. They look at each other, bow, begin to laugh, and arm in arm leave the hall. The rest of the students remain sitting.

Meditation seems to be based on restriction, and the old boys that I admired seemed to be living out of some free-flowing fountain that ignored what most of us thought of as necessary and real.

Which brings us to the flat tire.

The Flat Tire

I am in Michigan on the loaded-for-camping motorcycle, about to start the eight-hundred-mile trip home after a weekend with biker friends. It is four in the afternoon, and I am pulling out of the check-in lot for Ludington State Park, intending to spend the first night there before taking off.

As I accelerate through the gears, I notice a little drag every time I pull in the clutch; and then at fifty miles an hour, just before shifting to fifth, the front end begins to wobble rapidly. I pull in the clutch (never touch the brake when things like this happen), the bike loses speed too rapidly, and the back end is now oscillating like a bronco trying to throw its rider. I wobble to the side of the road, leaning it to the shoulder. I notice that there is a roaring noise and then realize that while I have squeezed the clutch, I am still holding the throttle jammed open. I let it go. Kill the engine. Get off the bike.

I have a flat tire. The hawk that rode the highway thermals squats crippled on the shoulder. The rear tire, nearly new, is squished. I say many foul things. Slam the seat. Kick a few rocks. Get out my phone. Call AAA. Get the promise of a tow truck. And then stand there, sick with fear.

Am I reacting to the terror of nearly being thrown from the bike? Not at all. If the tire could be fixed by magic, I would become calm and ride her off over the horizon. Near death or at least near severe road rash has not bothered me.

What is bothering me is that my plans have been disrupted. My picture of the future is in jeopardy. I may not get home five days from now for my regular oncology appointment. Seven days from now, I am scheduled to be the preacher at a St. Paul church. I might have to reschedule. I have reserved three campgrounds for the nights of my return trip. I have no chance of getting to them.

The task of getting the bike to a shop and getting the tire repaired moved on, but not with certainty. I was told that the odds of getting it repaired the next day were low, and I might lose as much as two days from my plans, or more if something really mechanically bad had gone wrong during the wobble to a stop. Given this information, my imagination was cooking up a storm of other disrupting possibilities. I slept badly and woke up sick to my stomach.

I was then, and still am, a student of meditation. I regularly meditate twice a day for half an hour. This meditation is a contemplation of my body, my feelings, my thoughts, and the phenomena around me. (Perhaps you recognize the four foundations of mindfulness as taught by the Buddha?) I not only do that on schedule, but also shift into that mode whenever an opportunity arrives or the situation seems to demand or even allow it.

Anxiety

At the same time, I am a very anxious guy. Casual acquaintances would not say so since I act calm under almost all circumstances. (Losing my temper at the flat tire was a rare indulgence.) However, I am always early, I always create negative scenarios, everything is always done much better than it needs to be done—and for all my personal appearance of sloppiness, all "i"s are dotted and all "t"s crossed. That is because I am a very anxious guy.

Now after the flat tire, with my anxiety filling me from groin to head. I really paid attention. I argued with myself about how stupid my feelings were and how likely it was that a huge motorcycle shop in the middle of an area filled with two-wheeling people would fix my flat quickly. This did not help at all. As rapidly as I created favorable scenarios, my imagination created negative scenarios. *More* rapidly actually. About a one positive to ten negative ratio.

John Cowan

Pictures

I focused on the bodily feeling, experiencing where the anxiety was functioning down there in groin and gut, and that helped the anxiety drop. But what really helped was to focus on my picture of the future, that which was being violated, and see if I could see that future as unnecessary. Indeed, could I devise alternative futures, such as renting a car and visiting friends in Kalamazoo, as worthy possibilities? This helped a lot. Not enough to make the feelings go away, but enough to make them livable. And enough to make me realize that my problem was that I was trapped by the pictures in my imagination. Instead of these pictures being alternate possibilities, one of them or two or three of them had become necessary for my well-being.

At two in the afternoon, my cell phone rang; it was the service manager at the shop telling me the bike was ready to roll. I picked it up and the next morning checked out of my emergency motel two days late heading for the Upper Peninsula. All bright and cheerful.

A few hours later, I was at a rest stop feeling anxious again. Not nearly as bad as with the flat, but still on the tense side. I was about to cross the Mackinac Bridge, and I had heard that some find the height unbearable. I was wondering if that might be me. I pictured myself frozen on the bridge, workmen gathering to help me over, fourteen women on Harleys laughing at me from the sidelines, my picture of myself as a competent rider destroyed.

Since the day before I had been playing with the "this bike will never be repaired" scenario, almost automatically I observed the picture of me being frightened on the bridge and accepted it as an interesting possibility, a new experience, one I might write about some day, or at least tell at late-night parties.

I had been gazing out on Lake Michigan, and suddenly everything became abnormally quiet and beautiful. I could count, I thought, the leaves on the shoreline trees. All I needed was the time. A guy was riding in on a motorcycle, and the shirt he was wearing was impossibly red and his jeans, although well worn, were impossibly blue. The green of the fir trees had just become iridescent. I realized that I loved this world in front of me, not passionately, but gently, and I realized that I was not at all anxious about anything. And it seemed unlikely that it was a coincidence that at this moment I had no picture in my imagination that demanded fulfillment.

That is when I decided to write this book.

Meditation for Motorcycle Drivers and Others Seeking Freedom

Something is up. There is a glorious way of being that is accessible to guys and gals who ride motorcycles, but it is not accessible in exactly the same way as it is to monks sitting in a garden in India denying themselves not only the motorcycle but also square meals, cell phones, sex, and violence. This way of being starts with the lessening of anxiety, but in so doing it does not deny imagination or its products and pleasures.

I think this is what the Buddha promised when he said that he could end suffering, and what Jesus offered when he recommended turning everything over to the Father and accepting the empire of God, which is right in front of us but we don't see it. Later followers of these two epochal figures have promised more and delivered less. I cannot offer you reincarnation at a higher level or a life of freedom from the wheel of *samsara* (the state of discontent) or resurrection after death in a heavenly kingdom. These might be available through the practices taught in the churches and the sanghas. Some say so.

I cannot offer you that. But, perhaps, I can help you deal with flat tires more calmly than I, and look forward to crossing the Mackinac Bridge. Perhaps I can offer you a significant step toward a bright and creative life. Perhaps I can offer you a mild *nirvana*, a world with much more light than you experience now, a peace that may not rival the peace that surpasses all understanding, but is pretty good in itself. And I am fairly convinced that all of this can be accessed in the middle of daily life, even the daily life of a guy negotiating the highways on a motorcycle.

Because this I have done.

The method will be to extend the practice of meditation to include the pictures you create in imagination and to observe the results of having these pictures: The feelings they cause. The intentions they attract. The activity they encourage. The anxiety they cause. The control they exercise.

At a campsite I was walking to the pump for water when I heard a car on the road behind me. I looked to my rear-view mirrors to see what was coming and then realized that since I was walking, I had no rear-view mirrors. I was so acclimatized to the bike that when on it I did not notice it, and when off it I could forget that I was not on it. A motorcycle is a complicated machine, yet with practice driving it can become so simple that the fact "driving" is occurring is not noticed.

In some ways, this is a complicated book. There is much to learn and organize. But after a while, this process can be second nature. By the end of the book, but not before, you will have some simple things to do that will allow you intentionally to change your dullest days to brightness and your most anxious, the days of *samsara*, to peaceful. Ultimately this is a simple trick of the mind, but to bring it off you need to know how memory and imagination and observation and anxiety and attraction and intention work together to draw you forward. If not understood, they plump you alive into an early grave, but if understood and observed, they open the vistas of the wonderful life.

You can be riding the motorcycle called "you" gracefully and with ease. Effortless, free and alive, as the hawk rises.

A Small Exercise

In every chapter I will ask you to practice a little. Not much. But the practice is important. You must experiment with *your* mind. Not just watch my mind at work. It's not my mind that is creating your well-being or your anxiety.

Think through one of your activities. Think about the pictures you create in imagination and see if you can feel how they pull you ahead. What happened that you ended up at the sink instead of the stove? Why did you decide to mow the lawn now? Not the reasons, but what was the picture in your head that got you out the door and how did it pull you? The height of the grass? The shine of the new mower? The bikini-wearing woman sunning next door? Why didn't you stop at the grocery store? What was the picture in your mind? Crowded checkout lines? Or the frozen dinner already in your freezer?

Play with it much as I have played with the memory of the flat tire. I would think you might find it interesting.

Chapter Two:
How You Became Anxious

How Anxious Are You?

Perhaps you do not think of yourself as anxious. Well then, let me tell you how anxious I am and see if any of the sources of my anxiety match up with yours.

I am afraid that:
- People will not like me.
- I will not have enough money.
- My motorcycle will break down in the middle of nowhere.
- It will rain before I can pitch my tent.
- My condo will go down in value. (It has.)
- My financial advisor has me in the wrong investments.
- The airplane my family or I is on will be hit by terrorists.
- My kids will lose their jobs.
- My wife will get sick.
- My cancer will return.
- I will be disrespected.
- This book will never be published. (Close.)
- I will die soon.
- I will die someday. (Probably.)

- The Chinese stock market will crash, and we will all go down. (Ahem.)
- Bird flu will happen.
- I will never again have anything interesting to do.
- I am not fulfilling my destiny.

This is from a seventy-three-year-old man who is well invested, has no children at home, and has a younger working wife.

Twenty years ago I was afraid of more:
- I would get fired. (Which happened.)
- I would not get a raise.
- I would be moved to another department with less meaningful work. (Happened.)
- The company would fail. (It did.)
- I would lose my leadership position in the department.
- The college fund would collapse. (It did.)
- My retirement fund would vanish. (Half of it did.)
- My children would be badly injured or succumb to a childhood disease.
- I would lose all my clients. (During my consulting days.)
- Somebody would be so angry with one of my sermons that they would quit the church. (During my pastoring days.)

Now that I have you started, could you create without too much trouble a similar list? I just sat down and typed this one without even trying. (Take a crack at it. It is not my anxiety but yours that we are trying to influence.)

To approach this another way: How often does the world appear to you a radiant place? How often do you feel a swelling of the heart? A wonder at the unlikelihood of life?

Anxiety blocks all other emotions. If you normally would say that you are feeling nothing, the odds are that you are always mildly anxious even if you are not feeling the anxiety. When teachers of meditation practice refer to a quiet mind, what they really mean is a mind not drowning in anxiety. Jesus said that anxiety was the big problem. He said it clearly: "Be not anxious …"

You are at a party and all these friendly people are bringing you no happiness, because you are concerned as the host or hostess that the party will not go "right" or you are worried as an invitee that people will not think you a fine person.

You are at the lakeshore and the sunset delights you not in the least, because you are planning how to get home and are anxious about the task.

You do not want to go to work because you are afraid you are not up to the job.

Or you do not want to go to work because there is a long meeting and it will be boring and you will do nothing to change that situation because you are afraid of the consequences of stepping out of your assigned role of a very nice person trying to be obedient and dutiful.

You can think of seven things that may go wrong tomorrow because you are an anxious person and anxious people imagine what can go wrong.

I took a colleague to the airport once and listened to him curse the airline for delaying his flight simply because there were severe thunderstorms in New York, where the flight was to land. He was so anxious to be on time, he did not mind if he arrived dead as long as he was punctual. He would never have said he had an anxious bone in his body. But he sounded anxious to me.

Why did the woman in the Lexus cut me off in traffic the other day? Judging from her blank-eyed expression over the top of her cell phone, she was too anxious about something else to see a motorcycle alongside her.

Some Causes of Anxiety

If you lived on an island in the South Pacific, I might believe that you were not anxious, but in this society I suspect you are. A woman I know who counsels cloistered (not talking, not allowed out of the walls) nuns says their primary problem is that they are so busy and therefore so anxious about being behind in their work that they cannot pray.

To compound matters, we live in a society where we are assured that there are no rules for our life, so we can attempt whatever we want. I cannot say I am a failure because I was forced to be a serf, or a carpenter, or a surgeon. I made all those decisions including my marriage, so if they are not working out, it is I that am responsible. In an earlier age, I could have at least blamed my social status for my job and my parents for my marriage. (Indeed, in some societies no one would ask if his or her marriage was working out. Being married is what you did, not what you chose in search of happiness.)

This should give us sufficient sources of anxiety. But for all that, could you and I not simply float by all these sources, ignoring their impact? We do not. We are easily hooked. Listing sources, while indicative of the likelihood of anxiety, does not answer the question: How did you *become* anxious?

How Did You Become Anxious?

You were not anxious as a baby. (Remember Jesus's admonitions about being like a little child if you want to enter the kingdom of heaven?) You may have come out of the womb hollering, but you were not anxious. Soon your instincts directed you to your mother's breast for all you needed in life, and then in a bit you learned that screaming some got your diaper changed. At the start it was all pretty much stimulus and response for fulfilling your basic needs.

Early on, the world became interesting to you starting with you yourself. You could grasp a toe and contemplate it for long periods of time. Put it in your mouth and suck on it to discover how it tasted. A rattle or a colored object on a string was a source of fascination. Simple awareness without the need to do anything productive was yours.

In his creeping stage, my firstborn began thumping his head on the floor. We took him to the pediatrician, who was intrigued but not at all alarmed. After studying the child in action for a while, the doctor pointed out that he was thumping his head on the rug, but if placed on linoleum he would not thump. His diagnosis? The kid was fascinated with the feel of head banging on rug. Which diagnosis held up nicely over the next couple of days, at which time head-banging ended, having been explored enough. (This particular son now owns several small businesses, which might indicate that head-banging continues. But he left a corporate job to do that, so at least he still avoids the linoleum.)

At the same time as this stage was tapering off, you began to realize that certain behavior brought you certain rewards. If you dropped a spoon from your high chair, you could watch someone retrieve it and place it in front of you. If they did not retrieve it quickly, you could scream and have the satisfaction of watching them obey and grumble at the same time. They might even wag a finger in your face, interesting in itself. And then if you cried, you might be picked up and hugged. Life was good.

(For most children in the set of people who read books like this, as a baby or toddler, expressing needs meant they were fulfilled. Some children in poverty or in situations of abuse learn early that expressing needs will not get them fulfilled. They give up on even crying. A moment please, you and I, to mourn for them. I am not joking. Never let a picture like that pass through your awareness without acknowledging the suffering. Unless you prefer being dead.)

Your memory recorded many things that you might want to have happen again or receive again. It recorded successful tactics and unsuccessful tactics. You began to develop imagination, the capacity to search your memory, bring out pieces of it, join them together, in old ways and new, to create an image of what you want, bring up alternative methods to get there, and then put it all into action.

You now were developing the ability to be intentional. Early on you responded to immediate needs. The hunger in you and the breast in front of you. But now you began to consider what you might have, and you developed a picture of it in your mind and the intention to have it.

You remember what shaking a rattle was like, you know that screaming got you the rattle in the past, so when you imagine having a rattle now, you are attracted to having it, you decide you want it, and you scream until some adult gets you the rattle or at least provides you something that makes you forget you wanted it.

You remember the taste of ice cream, and you remember that ice cream lives in restaurants, so when mommy takes you to a restaurant, you tend to imagine yourself eating ice cream and you know that saying "ice cream" emphatically may indeed produce ice cream, so you have the intention to have ice cream and you begin the process of turning up the volume until you get it.

You remember how happy your teacher was when you did your homework and how happy your parents were when you brought home an "A," so you see yourself basking in praise again and you exert yourself on homework.

Wearing the right dress gets you "in" with the "in crowd" in elementary school, which fits nicely your picture of happiness, so as a high school girl you diligently scan the teen magazines for what is the latest and work long hours after school to ensure you can afford to dress yourself according to the imagined picture of adolescent propriety.

When you first entered the job market, you sent out fifty resumes and in a month had ten interviews. Now that after two decades you have been let go by that company, you reach back into your memory for how it is done, and prepare fifty more resumes, to fulfill your imagined picture of being reemployed.

Starting very early in life, you developed a set of self-preserving strategies, tactics, and behaviors to get you what you wanted. You developed a picture of a preferred future, you intended to make it real, and then you went to work to get what you intended to have.

(I am talking to the dominant culture here. There are corners of it and vast segments of the dominated cultures that neither provide this skill nor have many models around of what it looks like. While some of them are quite proud of their cultures, many of them are quite hungry also.)

But over the years, as you have matured, things have changed, and your tactics have become less effective.

Shortly after you sat in the high chair, your success ratio began to drop precipitously. Aunt Mary was babysitting, and she would not pick up the spoon. Suddenly you had a hint that intending something and getting it was not automatic.

Mom grew angry and scooped you up and marched out of the restaurant. The teacher said the homework looked very neat, thank-you, but most of the problems were worked incorrectly. The "in crowd" could not care less what you were wearing—you were not going to be "in" anyway. And you already have figured out what happened to the second fifty resumes without my telling you. Perhaps you too have a memory of showering the world with unwanted paper?

Sometimes things played out the way you imagined them, but often they did not. Intending to make real your mental picture of the future was often the first step on the road to failure.

That is how you became anxious. From the moment when you realized that screaming might not get you the spoon, to the day you realized that the job hunt might not succeed, every time you imagined something you might want, you became anxious that you might not get it. (It is at this point that you and I leave most other meditation methodologies, for at this point they suggest you stop intending and stop imagining. Return to infancy. Do it well, and you will live in bliss. There are reports of a few people who have done it. Most who try are still not quite to first base.)

Now to add even further to the list of anxieties, think of all the possibilities laid open before you by the daily advertising barrage that if you choose to have, you might not get. Stand on any metropolitan corner in any middle-class neighborhood and observe all that could be yours but probably will not be, from vehicles to lawns to houses to spouses to children to physical shape—the list rolls on endlessly. If for but a moment your imagination pictures even one of these as desirable, your anxiety level rises, at least slightly. It depends on how seriously you want it and how difficult it might be to obtain.

How to free yourself from anxiety?

Can a Layperson Be a Monk?

The Buddha said that "desire" was the source of suffering and if you would desire nothing, you would not suffer. (Sometimes the word for "desire" is translated as "clinging," which makes the advice slightly easier, but for our purposes pretty much the same.) Only recently have western laypeople attempted to follow the precepts of the Buddha, and they are having their difficulties. How does one live as a layperson working in the world, and not desire? Indeed, if you hope to get things done, you not only desire, you cling. The anxiety that rises from this uncertainty is what fuels the activity that gets you what you imagined and intended to achieve.

As a consultant, I worked from my own home. Friends would ask how I could put nose to grindstone when so many other possibilities were in front of me: sitting on the deck, reading a novel, turning on the TV. My answer was that I had an intention that my family would be financially solvent. I was far from certain that I would make that image reality. The anxiety produced by the gap drove me to not only work during the workweek, but also work late at night, and on weekends, and during holidays.

I speak with the confidence of a person who has program-managed a couple of million-dollar programs and several one-hundred-thousand-dollar ones in a corporate setting. During those years, if I had not clung tightly to my imagined outcome, I never would have achieved it. And because of that clinging, I was often extremely anxious. Which drove me to shout, rage, weep, smile, threaten, and eventually produce the product I was being paid to produce.

As a candidate for the Roman Catholic priesthood, I was trained to be a monk, free from anxiety. As a layperson, I had to learn a different way of being. Painful, but effective.

D. T. Suzuki, the person most responsible for introducing the theories of Zen to the United States, and Thomas Merton, the Trappist monk most responsible for popularizing them in our culture, were engaged in a written conversation about the desert fathers, early Christian hermits. One story they debated was:

> A group of hermits invited some travelers to stay overnight. In the morning they discovered that the travelers had taken off with all of the hermits' worldly goods, not much to start with. The hermits hunted the thieves down and turned them over to the police. Concerned about whether or not they had done the hermit-like thing, they went to a very old hermit who lived a short way off and told him the story. He chewed them out for being bad hermits.

Suzuki thought the old man wrong, for as Suzuki said: "Thieves should be put in prison."

Merton thought the old man right, for as he said: "Thieves should be put in prison, but monks should not put them there."

Monks should neither desire nor cling. They should not have cared in the least that a few plates and spoons and a robe or two went out the door. That job belongs to laypeople who need those plates for their children's supper, with all the anxiety that goes with it. That is why the Caucasian Buddhist of the west has trouble with the Buddha: He is trying to be both monk and layperson at once.

Christianity does not have precisely this problem. True, Jesus said: "Blessed are you who have become poor to follow me." But within a few years after his death, most Christians ignored that in favor of having lots of stuff and being anxious. Of course, they do not experience the kingdom of light promised by Jesus, but at least they have a membership in a golf club.

A Layperson's Path to Bliss

So is there a road out of this suffering for the normal person, the program manager, the nurse, the mother, the clinical psychologist, the governor, the army sergeant, all of us folk who are expected to keep the world running, want a few things in return, but would prefer to be able to see the world with the interest, joy, and clarity we lost back there in the first few months of life?

I think we can at least come close. The key will be to learn to observe and love the process of imagining possibilities, intending accomplishment, experiencing anxiety, working, accomplishing, and as we observe the process, use it with care.

Those who have sought to relieve anxiety have done it by denying the imagination. Don't desire, don't cling, be poor, do not imagine a better future for yourself in general, and certainly do not intend to accomplish the specifics of it—and you will not be anxious.

However, you will walk around with your eyes cast down and your hands folded, you will accept the October chill in your room without complaint, and you will contribute no new and useful thing to our collective lives, and thieves will steal whatever they want from you with impunity, which is neither good for you nor for them.

You will wimp out. You will lose what freedom you have. You will passively sign up for a motorcycle ride across the country with one hundred others, surrendering your wickedly beautiful machine and its road-eating desire to a line of the similarly enthralled boring their way down the interstate slab. Nothing imagined or pursued except the back fender of the bike in front of you.

The hawk will march down the freeway.

I think that unnecessary. You can live without anxiety as a contemplative and be a creator of good things for yourself and others at one and the same time. The path will be to understand the pictures in your imagination, the anxiety they create, and the effect of observing all that process in operation.

A Small Exercise

Pay attention to your anxiety. Not an easy task because it is so much a part of you.

I once lived on a busy corner, and in the summer I was accustomed to napping just before supper with the windows open, the breeze alleviating the summer heat. One day I woke up in panic. Something was radically wrong. I looked around the room, out in the hall. Finally, I looked outside to realize that there were no vehicles waiting at the corner semaphore. For the first time in five years, my room was silent.

That is the case with your anxiety. If you did not have it, you would think you were in heaven and might have a panic attack besides. That happens all the time when perhaps as a result of meditation practice or as a result of dumb luck, anxiety ends for a moment and the world appears in its natural radiance.

But for now, the exercise is simple. Just notice your anxiety. Don't get mad at yourself for it. Do not try to make it go away. Just observe it.

Orientation

Up to now we have looked at the moments in my life that led up to writing this book (first chapter), and (second chapter) we have explored the process of becoming anxious, all in service to developing a method for being awake and non-anxious while living an active, free, and creative life. Next (third chapter) comes an overview of how this can work.

At the same time, I have asked you to perform some tiny exercises. I am hoping that you will find this book not simply interesting but perhaps life changing. Tiny exercises? Please.

Whose mind are we tinkering with?

Chapter Three:
The Creative Anxiety Model

The Problem We Are Solving

When the Buddha told his followers that they would be able to wake up if they would sit still and meditate, they asked him, "Meditate on what?"

He could have said: "Observe everything." But instead he said: "Contemplate the body, the feelings, thoughts, and phenomena."

In case you haven't noticed, that was everything! But it did help to have some categories to subdivide everything. And now I say that you can contemplate in action, and to do that you should contemplate everything that is happening in action. And you, as did the Buddha's followers, might say: "Everything is too much. Break it into pieces."

Unlike the Buddha, I will not give you pieces that cover everything, but I will cover the big bases. They are: Imagining, intending, anxiety, and then observing itself. Since these four functions work together, I will give them to you as a model. I call it the "Creative Anxiety model." Following it leads to soaring through life on the wings of your desire as anxiety free as the hawk overhead.

Definitions

A model is a representation of how something works. The model I provide, as most models, does not cover every attribute of your life. That would be too complex for this simple book. Multitudes of models exist, and they will point up things about yourself that this model cannot. What the Creative Anxiety model does is provide a method for reducing your anxiety, seeing the world in beauty, and living a creative life. A tall order in itself.

This model will provide you a new way to order and understand what you observe passing through your mind, an explanation not for the person in stillness, the monk, but an explanation for the person in motion, the layperson.

Some of the thinking in this chapter is taken from the field of psycho-cybernetics, begun in the 1940s and quite popular in self-help books and management courses since then. I differ slightly from them in that they are oriented not to increasing your well-being but to increasing your accomplishments. They do not care how anxious you feel as long as it drives you to receiving the Pulitzer Prize. I am hopeful that I can help you keep moving forward and live a life of light and joy while doing so.

Some of the thinking in this chapter is taken from the field of Gestalt psychology. Gestalt psychology was written with therapeutic change as the objective. Indeed, Fritz Perls, one of the founders, was amazed and confounded when he accidentally found himself in the Kingdom of Light. Although its existence is a reasonable outcome of the therapy he was working with, it never occurred to him it was there, and he did not understand it when he found himself delighting in it. Fortunately he wrote it down before he forgot it.

Some of the thinking in this chapter is taken from Buddhist philosophy and Christian mystical practice, with a major difference. Contemplative practice generally reveres the child that you once were, simple awareness of reality, and would like you to return to that way of being. In pursuit of that end, teachers describe all the later functions of your being in pejorative terms.

One such writer calls all the other functions "the golem," a reference to a constructed and dangerous alter ego. For him, the later functions—wanting, willing, strategizing, acting, imagining—are all a monster best ignored for the real life, which is simple awareness. I admit myself in another book to using the term "persona" and the term "self" to set these functions aside as less important, and if not a monster at least a bit of a nuisance.

I am suggesting a radically different path with the Creative Anxiety model. In the model, while we will tend to identify with the first function we developed, the observing function, all of the others will remain ours and healthy and delightful and necessary to being human. Not for us a desiccated existence. We are creative people. Our creativity is not an extra, but part and parcel of the whole. Even having a certain kind and level of anxiety is seen as a necessary part of the human process. It is the price tag for freedom.

However, there is a problem in being this freedom-seeking person. The problem we presently have with our multiple functions is that they have careened out of control and are creating not an anxiety in service of the whole process but a debilitating anxiety, an anxiety run amok. Our multiple functions are accomplishing much less than they could with more effort than is needed.

Our intent here will be to get our functions of observing, picturing, and intending, settled down and pulling together in good order so that the anxiety they create is freedom producing and not dysfunctional, and that the anxiety is minimal, or even at times absent. To do this, we must have a sense of how these functions work together when they are a coordinated system.

The Creative Anxiety Model

1. The first function is "observing." I am capable of being aware of what is happening in my body, my feelings, my

thoughts, and the world around me. So I observe, and I appreciate what is.
2. As an adult I have memories. I am able to combine these memories in various ways to construct possible futures. This function I call "imagining." I will also refer to it as "picturing."
3. When I use my imagining to construct possible futures, the most attractive of these pictures will cause me to desire to make it real. The ability to desire a particular outcome is one of my functions. I will refer to this function as "feeling-response." I am attracted to or repelled by the imagined image. This is at one and the same time a feeling and a response. When it rises to the point to provoke action, it is called an "intention."
4. As soon as I have decided that a future is one that I want to make real, as soon as I have an intention, I experience "anxiety" because until I do make it real, I have failed. The level of this anxiety will vary depending on the importance to me of the outcome and the difficulty of the path to the outcome. I will refer to this anxiety as "creative anxiety" to distinguish it from pathological anxiety.
5. This creative anxiety drives me to work to close the gap between my ideal future and my present reality. The greater the anxiety, the greater I am driven. I am "acting."
6. To the extent I am able to observe this process at work, to that extent the functions in the process will organize themselves to produce the future with minimal creative anxiety.
7. To the extent that I live without anxiety, even creative anxiety, to that extent life will be peaceful and calm and the world will seem trustable, bright, and illuminated with glory.

Examples

Let us say that I sit at my computer and I stop typing for a moment to observe my surroundings and myself. I notice that I have stopped because the image of the words I want to type is fading and being replaced by another image, a cup of tea. The picture of the cup of tea becomes more specific, and I notice that I am drawn toward it and experience a slight unrest that I do not have it. I develop an intention to have it. I move into acting, go upstairs, prepare the cup, and return to my keyboard gently content.

Getting tea is a small cycle, not at all momentous, but indicative of the way it can be. Gentle. It could have been otherwise. I could have sat at the keyboard trying to surmount the temporary stoppage of the flow of words. I could have cursed the temptation to go upstairs. I could have banged out in misery fourteen more paragraphs, trying to stomp on what I really wanted to do. I could have been filled with the creative anxiety to get tea, and by refusing to let the accompanying intention take over and the necessary work occur, been trapped in that anxiety.

The writing would have been second-rate, and therefore the creative anxiety associated with creating a good product would have also been rampant. By failing to go with the flow, I would have plunged myself into an anxiety pit and accomplished little.

It is important to note, there would have been days when I would have plowed on, for in my observing of the situation, there would have been a client waiting tomorrow who would not pay me unless a certain number of pages was on her desk at a certain time. And then I would have been very conflicted, but at least if I observed, I would have known what I was conflicted about, and that too would have helped my overall system sort things out.

Now let us say that I am sitting in my motel room and my motorcycle is in an unknown repair shop and the service manager has explained that my flat tire may or may not be fixed soon. Without any trouble, I note the clouds of anxiety wafting through my body. They alert me to the need to either act or explore further. I know that acting will be counterproductive. The service manager will become annoyed, and in his annoyance I will move down his list of priorities. I decide to explore further.

I check what it is that my imagining is producing. There are several "negative" (in the sense that I do not want them to become reality) scenarios playing out. For example, I am in Ludington forever. I spend meaningless days sitting in front of my tiny room. I have to walk my legs off even to get to lunch. But in the midst of this mess is one "positive" scenario (that is the one that I want to occur). I insist that my present plan will not be violated. That I will remain on schedule. I will be home when I said I would. That is my intention, and the level of anxiety it is creating because of its impossibility is killing me. I am trapped by my imagination. I am limited. I am not free.

Once that most salient fact emerges, I follow my wife's telephoned advice and begin to construct alternative scenarios. To do so, I pull from my remembering what she would do based on my memories of her, since my memories of myself pretty much are of me stuck on my original intentions, come hell or high water.

(My ordination to the Roman Catholic priesthood resulted from sticking to an imagined outcome for twelve years without ever seriously imagining any other course. For this reason, I am the perfect author for this book because what is happening to you in small type, I have lived through in bold print and capital letters. One of the problems the great teachers of the past may have had is that their understanding came so swiftly that they did not quite know what they were doing. Some of the coaches who win the most were never that good as players. They know what "wrong" feels like. I assure you this teacher knows what "wrong" feels like. Whenever you find yourself saying, "Well, I am not as sick as the author," know that I agree with you. I think you will still find this very useful, just not as useful as I find it.)

Hawk Rising

So I begin to see myself doing what Edie might: renting a car, going to the local information center, discovering all the local sights, and spending a couple of days wandering an area that most people pay good money to visit.

Then I think what my son Ben might do, and I note that the U-Haul dealer is across the street and I can see in his lot several small trucks and at least one trailer on which the bike could be carried nicely. I enjoy driving my motorcycle more than anything, but I enjoy driving generally, and I find it interesting to drive a different vehicle. So this picture provides a plausible route for my anxiety-driven energies. I will rent a truck and trailer and haul the bike home.

And then I think of what my son Dave might do, and that rises to the top of the list of pictures. My feeling-response is so positive, it turns to an intention. I walk a quarter-mile to Walgreen's, buy a fun mystery novel, and park myself under the second oldest beech tree in Michigan. The U-Haul and the rental car remain simmering on the back burners, but for now I have a satisfactory image to replace the one that was driving me nuts, meeting the old schedule, and it also fulfills my picture of myself as a penurious being. For $2.25 (secondhand book), I have cured my problem.

I am still mildly anxious because I have a problem with anxiety, but the level is cranked down to medium-low instead of high-high. I am now a free man presently turned to accomplishing one picture, reading a book, but not trapped in it as a necessary scenario.

When my cell phone rings two hours later with the news that my bike is repaired, I experience momentary regret that I might not find time to fulfill my deepest intention and finish the novel.

By then I was so comfortable, my anxiety so low, that despite the fact there was still traveling time left in the day, I decided to pick up the bike, break in the new tire, go to supper, finish the novel, sleep the night, and roll in the morning. When I woke I had shed so thoroughly the thought that I must meet schedule that I even searched out a Ludington noted breakfast spot and took the time for a waffle and bacon before hitting the road.

Scan the above few paragraphs that tell the stories and see how the component parts of the Creative Anxiety cycle play out:
1. Observing
2. Remembering/Imagining
3. Feeling-Response leading to Intention
4. Creative anxiety
5. Acting
6. Self-Organizing
7. Bliss

In my work as a corporate program manager, my next few months would start with a vague notion from someone way up the corporate chart that we should have a computer-based education course on some subject, to use one actual case, the measurement of productivity.

As I left his office, my anxiety was surging through the roof because neither he nor I had any idea what he would find satisfying. The picture was an empty frame with no details.

Since I had no knowledge in the area and three other related projects to manage in which I did have a detailed picture and I did have knowledge, I pulled together a team of knowledgeable people under a manager who habitually got things done smartly. In a month his team turned up with the answer. I, and my client, were barking up the wrong tree.

While productivity at a divisional or company level could be measured, there was no point in teaching people at the working level how to do that. What could they do with the information? What was needed was a set of measurement tools to be applied at the work level. And they already existed.

Unfortunately they existed as translated from the Japanese and used examples foreign to our company and had Japanese thought patterns. (The Japanese apparently can refer to a concept and not explain it for ten chapters and expect the reader to hold that blank space ready until they fill it.)

So I went to my client and said, "We need the contents of this Japanese book, with examples from our industry, rewritten in plain English, in the form of several pamphlets, and genuinely different enough from the original that we are in an ethically alright position and most certainly safe from being sued."

This became our imagined picture and was given to one of our vendors, who experienced great anxiety, much of it creative, for a year or so, enormous activity, and a delightful product. I must admit that calm observing did not occur, nor much bliss. The vendor manager said to me that she would deeply appreciate it if after a morning meeting, she did not return to her desk to discover that I had called her every half-hour and that when she called back, I had forgotten what I had called about.

What can I say? I did not practice meditation then, and since then she has gone on to be paid huge salaries, have magnificent titles, and lead a happier life. Perhaps being around me then made everything easier in the future. I can hope.

Oh, and the pamphlets were pretty good, but one of my colleagues whose habitual imaginings included good-looking materials took over the project and made everything quite wonderful. A cycle I had found satisfying and complete roused his creative anxiety when compared to his pictures of complete. Hallelujah!

The Hawk

Watch a rising hawk. After a few awkward beats of powerful wings, he finds a thermal, an updraft, and rests upon it, rising, and then moves from one thermal to another into the sky, without effort. His sister, the crow, beats her way through life, struggling from point to point.

The pictures in our mind are the cliffs and clouds and sun by which thermals are formed. The feeling-responses and intentions are the thermals on which we shall rise. It is calm observation that allows us to see and manage our path among the thermals, and it is our creative anxiety that leads us to take those few powerful wing beats that lead us into this process.

With grace and power, we float.

A Way for You to Practice

I am not trying to map out everything about you with this model. I am trying to extend the practice of contemplative meditation from simply being aware and appreciative of body, feelings, thoughts, and phenomena in a retreat setting to being aware of self-in-motion, creating, doing, worrying, in order that bliss not be confined to the hermitage or to the monastery but can be carried into the office and factory and experienced by free people doing the world's work.

Would you now apply this?

1. Take a breath or two and notice your body, how you are sitting and breathing. Look around to see if there is anything interesting to do. Since this is an experiment, you need not discover anything important; indeed, perhaps it would be best if it were something small. Raise or lower the shade. Turn the light off or on. Make a cup of coffee.

2. Whatever you decide on, for the sake of this experiment, do not do it immediately. If you do it immediately, you will not experience the cycle. Allow an image to form of you doing whatever you have chosen. See the shade pulled, the light on, the coffee made. When you do anything, this imaging of an agreeable future happens but usually so quickly you do not notice.

3. Sharpen your focus on that picture until it becomes that which you most want to do in life right now. Observe it until you have a feeling-response of attraction to it. Stare at it until a definite intention to do it forms.

4. Allow yourself to feel the deep pull, the anxiety within you, to get to the job and do something. Since this is a

small task, the pull will be small, but it is there. Sit with it for a while.
5. Then act slowly. As a film in slow motion, allow your acting to unreel. The shade moves slowly. The switch unfortunately just clicks, but crossing to it can be slow and deliberate, and observing the change in light can continue with two or three flicks of the switch, but slowly. The coffee making can become a series of imagined images, each action held in abeyance until the anxiety rises.
6. Continue to observe the anxiety drop as the gap between image and reality closes.
7. Continue to observe until you are experiencing peace and brightness in this small and specific activity.

If in the course of trying this, you are prevented by some other image that is beyond the experimental and perhaps even necessary in this moment, such as answering the door, going to the bathroom, or answering the phone, see if you can observe the Creative Anxiety process while doing that.

If this all proves too hectic, then try again in a quieter time. Do not be hard on yourself. After all, the great contemplatives of the past were alone in a corner of the forest and trying to limit their distractions. On our path to contemplation in the midst of activity, we must start with at least the quieter activities.

Indeed, much of life will be spent pulled into the non-observing functions. As I type, I have half-hour-long bursts of imagining pictures that are not yet on the page and the anxiety rising to make the page match the mind and the activity pouring out of my fingers as the page emerges, and then, only then, pause to experience myself at this table, hands on this keyboard, the imagining cooling, but splendidly aware, content, and most happy, thank-you.

I have to go upstairs and get myself an orange to celebrate the beauty of this moment. but as we go forward. will you return to this small exercise off and on during the day? Maybe five times a day? It is fun and relaxing. Really. I am on my way upstairs to do it now. The image of that orange is taking over.

The next chapters will add information to each step in the Creative Anxiety model. As you learn, incorporate the understandings into your practice. The Buddha encouraged his followers to experiment for themselves. He only asked that the student try his ideas. So I can do no less. Just try what I am offering. See if it works for you.

Gotta go! Orange! Stair-climbing! Gotta! I am getting very anxious.

Orientation

Up to now we have looked at the moments in my life that led up to writing this book (first chapter), and (second chapter) we have explored the process of becoming anxious, all in service to developing a method for being awake and usefully anxious while living a free, active, and creative life (third chapter.) We will now pull out the microscope and look in-depth at each step in the process.

At the same time, I have asked you to perform some tiny exercises. I am hoping that you will find this book not simply interesting but perhaps life changing. Tiny exercises? Please. Whose mind are we observing? I have done this for years, so it's your turn.

The Second Parable: The Disappearing Puppet

Once there were twenty-three dancing puppets. One of them took off her strings and marched off the stage. The others stopped their dancing for a moment of stunned shock, and then they built an altar and worshipped her.

Chapter Four: Pictures

Pictures Defined

When I say "picture," I am not necessarily referring to a drawing. At times that might be the case, but usually a picture is some sense of what might become reality. In the case of moving your pen from one corner of the desk to the other, I doubt if a full-fledged picture of the pen in the new corner would rise in your mind. Most likely your eyes would begin to rotate to the corner, a flash of semi-sight would pick up a not even complete picture of the pen, and the pen would be there before the picture had even formed.

I had a sense of having a new tire replace my flat tire, but the motivating picture was the picture of me back on schedule, and if you insisted that I tell you precisely what was in my mind, I suspect it was some combination of me pulling the bike into the garage, my wife greeting me, Ludington a distant memory, and the words "on time" printed in block letters. Often the picture is fuzzy.

Sometimes it is so simple, as in "far" or "close." As I am caught halfway around a truck by an oncoming car, my "picture" is simply "safety" as I jam on the brakes. Most likely I will duck behind the truck, but at least once I ran off onto the opposite shoulder. That was not the plan, and I had no picture of doing it until the last second. That turned out to be the one place safety was at.

Sometimes the pull is simply toward. I will eat the apple. How more "toward" can I get? Lovers often try to eat each other in their effort to go toward. Insane as that is, it is also normal, as anyone trying to hide a hickey can testify. A detailed picture, including the resulting embarrassment, would have prevented the bite from happening. Maybe.

So "picture" is a fuzzy word.

There are three types of pictures: Operational Pictures, Cultural Pictures, and Self-Preserving Pictures.

Operational Pictures

Operational pictures are the pictures I create when I want to accomplish something. The picture in my imagination of riding a motorcycle when I am deciding to buy one motivates me to walk into the shop. The picture I had of a perfect motorcycle as derived from experiences as a young man, leads me as an old man to buy a midsize bike stripped of accessories instead of the full dresser I could afford and which in many ways would have been more suited to the long distances I plan to ride.

Vancouver Island first becomes an interesting dot on a map. And then I read about it, and it exerts a pull to come. And then I explore possible campgrounds and see on the Internet pictures of the KOA thirty-five miles above Victoria, and I am hooked. I have a clear picture of my bike in front of a Kamping Kabin, on that island, and two thousand some miles must be conquered to make that picture come true. Four months of planning and charting and purchasing, and then five days of riding, three of them across the bare and empty western plains bored to freaking death, and all because I have that picture embedded in my imagination and I will not let go.

When I sit at my computer, I have an operational picture of a completed chapter filling the space now occupied by nothing.

When I was a home-based consultant, my friends would ask me how I could avoid turning on the television or reading a book or dozing on the back porch. Simply, I had an operational picture of my family continuing to eat and my sons attending college. In the fragile world of consulting, he who dozes dies. A very useful creative anxiety drove me to work to complete that picture.

Many pictures are of other people. Perhaps you see yourself maintaining a friendly relationship with someone. Or the presence of another person creates in you the urge to cause them to smile or to laugh. Perhaps you see some people as hungry and are willing to devote large portions of your life to see them fed.

An operational picture need not be of a physical thing.

Operational Long-Term and Short-Term Pictures

You will form pictures of long-term hopes, visions, and goals. They are exceedingly important for consistency and motivation over months and years. A monk, particularly one housed in a monastery, need not worry about such. St. Francis wanted his friars to beg just enough for the day, and after sleeping in the woods overnight, he expected them to start fresh in the morning. Long-range goals promote anxiety.

However, you are a layperson and therefore need them or your family will not thrive, and even if you are single your landlord still requires the rent. Once Francis died, the Pope required that Franciscans start thinking of the future. Nor did they argue much.

However, long-range goals do promote anxiety and must be held gently, as much as possible without clinging if you hope to live in freedom. If you will take the long goals and break them down until you are at that which is needed to be done right now, or at least right today, they may promote some light.

Once they are in place and your time is blocked out productively, then you can focus on the immediate, and in that focus you can experience freedom from anxiety and you can experience the kingdom of brightness.

I want to write a book, a long-range goal that will keep me directed over a year, and bring me back to my computer time after time. I may or may not succeed at that. I care only slightly. Today I am working on a chapter. This I can probably do. The time is available. Anxiety softens.

Now I sit in front of the machine. Decide to open it up. Bring Word to the desktop. Now I type the chapter heading. Now I begin the first paragraph. And now I am working on short-term pictures and am feeling no anxiety and some delight.

I need a task requiring less intelligence to really float off into *nirvana*, but this is not bad.

Cultural Pictures

One of the difficulties in marketing a meditation course or in marketing a meditation book is convincing anyone they need it. The purpose of Creative Anxiety is to wake up to the process flowing inside you. Most people have no idea that they are asleep.

Charlie gets up in the morning, eats his cereal, drinks his coffee, puts on his suit, gets into his Toyota, goes to the office, works through his papers, attends his meetings, greets people, makes decisions, returns home, and makes it through the entire day without having a moment of conscious activity.

If he is not aware of his own existence as he piddles through the day, how can he do anything?

He is on autopilot!

As a family, a small group of people, a company, or a nation, begin the process of growth, in order that there be good order and progress they evolve a set of rules. While some may get codified, most are unwritten. These unwritten rules are called cultural norms. From infancy you have been taught the correct way to do things. The result is that you do not need to be awake. Most of life can be lived following the directions of your autopilot programmed with cultural norms. You are not free! You are trapped into doing what everyone does.

There is a law (a codified cultural norm) that when driving a car, you pass oncoming traffic to their left. There is not a law that when walking you walk to the left of the person approaching you on the sidewalk. But there is a cultural norm. In the United States when hugging, you place your right ear by the other person's right ear. Try it otherwise, and you may bump noses. Try it. I dare you.

A friend of mine at church complimented me on my willingness to drive a shabby, rust-eaten, ten-year-old van despite the fact that others thought it weird. I was unaware that my penuriousness was violating a norm, and once so informed I went out and bought a new vehicle before I moved to my next parish assignment. And when I left that parish, the master of ceremonies for my going-away party commented on how I was a good pastor even if I drove a pickup truck.

As you walk through life, the culture presents pictures of the way it should be done. On the other hand, to be alive, free, and awake, you must go through the cycle of allowing alternative pictures to arise in your imagination, wait for your feeling-response to form toward one of them, and then intend and do an action. When, daily, picture after picture arises from the cultural memory without alternatives and you act without waiting or discerning where your feelings lie, you are asleep. You are living a life without intention.

And most people are ordinarily asleep. What seems to be an intention, as they climb the corporate ladder, or carry the burdens of social work, or drive their children from one event to another, is not intention but slavish response to what the culture says should be done. Why do so many regret their corporate lives? They were slaves even when they thought they were pursuing their own ambitions, for even the ambition was not theirs but a product of the culture.

As you move through the rest of today, would you simply try to be aware of when you are following a cultural picture without thinking or feeling? Just say to yourself:

- This cup of coffee is being drunk because everybody is supposed to need a cup of coffee in the morning, not because I am thirsty for coffee or feel any chemical draw to it.
- This is not my kind of car, but it fits what a person with my salary should drive.
- I am in church, but I don't enjoy church. I am in church because it is the thing to do.
- I am talking about football because us guys are supposed to like the stupid sport.
- I am answering this question because it would be impolite not to.
- I am working my butt off to be selected for a job I will not enjoy.
- I am desperately trying to get my weight down until I can wear the jeans I wore as a teenager.

Play this game a bit, and you will be surprised at how far you can go in a day without a self-chosen and conscious impulse.

Be very careful about doing anything to change this. Skip the cup of coffee if you will. That should not be too difficult. Try going to a house party and skipping a drink. That is much more difficult. An associate of mine would claim that he was an alcoholic when he went to parties. It would scare the hostess off his back. If he simply said he did not want to drink, she and her husband would hand him a beer anyway to make certain that everyone was experiencing happiness the way the culture said happiness was to be experienced.

Why the panic when someone breaks cultural norms?

The great enforcer of cultural norms is the expectation that if everyone will do what the culture demands, everyone and everything will be all right. In particular, if I obey the cultural norms, I will not die.

Why does the driver who had the green light go into shock when struck by the driver running the red? He was doing what the culture (as codified law in this case) said he should, and despite his conformity he was not all right. The world as he knows it is falling apart. His trust in the workings of the universe has been totaled along with his vehicle.

In my early thirties, I was walking with a friend. Suddenly he looked up, pointed at the sky, exclaimed about something up there, and then fell writhing on his back, face contorted. An hour later I left the emergency room and had difficulty walking upright. My universe had fallen apart. I had lost my confidence in everything, including which way was "up." I was doing a perfectly normal thing and expected that as long as I did what one should, my companion would not throw a fit. One of the reasons I was able to be upright is that I never doubted that it was easy. Suddenly I realized that going from upright to writhing on the boulevard was simple and ordinary and eminently possible.

If I do what the culture says, everything should be all right. And among the "all rights" is that I should live on forever. The culture guarantees eternal life. Not out loud, of course. No one would ever believe that. But by implying that the right way of doing things will keep everything running forever.

As we walk through daily life in our delusion that we will be permanent if the culture is maintained, how do we react to someone who is not maintaining the culture? Very negatively! At an unconscious level, we feel they are rocking the boat, risking our very lives.

That is why my van and my pickup truck require forgiveness, and that is why Jesus needed crucifixion.

Six well-known Muslim clerics were arrested in the Minneapolis–St. Paul airport for suspicious behavior. They were praying. Obviously any Muslim doing that in that place is a dangerous person. If they had been Christian, they would have just been thought nuts. Unless they were clergy or even bishops, and then it would be inappropriate but understandable.

Be very careful with these cultural pictures. Be sly in seeking alternatives outside them. Your neighbor is asleep and, if wakened, much like a person struggling with blankets, as he is aroused may hurt you.

Self-Preserving Pictures

How often do we interrupt this creative process by saying: "I can't do that. It is just not me."

What does this "not me" mean?

As you progress through life, you accumulate in memory pictures of yourself thinking, feeling, imagining, acting. This activity is a product, we feel, of ourselves. Because I am who I am, this is what I have done and therefore I can look at what I have done and know who I am, and that who I am limits me from doing other than what I have done. This is what I am capable of—what I have done.

But ...

What if it works the other way? What if who I am is a product of what I have done and have remembered? That *is* the way it works. The self is your remembered self. And it is your remembered self acting. So if you want to change the self, just do something different.

Many years ago, I used to run a workshop that created enormous psychological change. Those who attended were asked to identify a way of acting that was "they" and then do something different. Not something huge, just something different.

A forty-year-old housewife spent the night dancing with a twenty-year-old college student. She entered that event dowdy and poured out of it sensuous.

My sister, who hates conflict, turned off the television in the middle of the Super Bowl. (That turned out to be risk-free because it was halftime, but she did not know that.)

Passive-aggressive Frank spent the days confronting everyone who annoyed him. When he returned to work, his colleagues had to make more space in the office's emotional system for the new Frank.

When they did something truly different, they found that their sense of self began to disintegrate. At the same time, in the moment they formed an intention to no longer slavishly respond to the picture of who they were yesterday, they found themselves acting from some deeper place in their very being.

A few years before I taught this workshop, I had come to it as a participant after twelve years in a seminary and five as a parish priest. During the session, I spent my days expressing feelings I do not express and my nights tossing in bed trying to explain to myself who I was if I could do this. I discovered that many others in the workshop were not at all impressed with me as a tower of strength, but were more likely to describe me as, perhaps I was not hearing right, pathetic. There, that was some new information to integrate.

A couple of weeks after the close of the workshop, I told the course guru that it was like being asked to pull one pin and then finding out that all the pins were interwoven and pulling one collapsed them all.

There is the grip of the self-preserving picture. ("Get a grip on yourself.") In your depths, you know that pulling one pin will pull them all. So when someone asks you if you would sing in the choir, you say that you do not sing. The truth is that you did not sing in the past and you are afraid of what else might be true if you try and succeed at doing it now.

Here is an exercise:
1. List three things you do all the time.
2. Next to each of them, write one small thing you could do that would be different.
3. Rank them in order of difficulty.
4. Do the easiest.

If I were to do this exercise, the three things I do all the time would be:
1. Listen to others without interruption.
2. Entertain clerks.

3. Support people's versions of the truth in casual conversation.

In order of increasing difficulty, the different behaviors would be:
1. Ignore clerks.
2. Argue with others' versions of the truth.
3. Interrupt others.

Most people to whom I have offered this exercise say that simply identifying alternatives causes anxiety beyond what they expected. As it should. It is your very sense of self that is being tinkered with.

Could you list for yourself ten self-preserving pictures you carry around that impact your behavior? You might want to review them for what should go on the discard list, what on the alter list, and what on the cherish list.

Cultural Pictures and Self-Preserving Pictures

As you become more and more awake, notice not only the operational picture toward which you are striving but notice also the cultural pictures and self-preserving pictures limiting and proscribing your steps toward those goals and raising your level of anxiety.

When I thought I would die confronted with a flat tire, it was indeed an operational difficulty I faced: I could not get home on schedule. But the reason it was a gut-wrenching difficulty was my self-preserving picture of myself as someone who is always on schedule and in control of my own destiny.

As a child, I lived in an era and in a house where children did what their parents asked without complaint. Even as a young man, while I no longer obeyed or felt obligated to obey, I did feel obligated to listen to my parents' comments and suggestions with respect. My father rained down on me his negative judgments on my actions. I bought the wrong car. I wore the wrong clothes. I smoked (as did he). I should have done this, and I should have done that.

When I was thirty, he commented in passing on my sideburns. They were too long. He walked on into the dining room, and I followed him, turned him around, lifted him by his shirt off the ground, pinned him against a wall, and very firmly told him I had had enough and I would not be in his house again.

I turned with an immense sense of freedom and headed for the door. My mother stopped me, begged me to stay, and I did. She asked me to apologize to my father, and I did.

And as I did, I physically felt compression around my head and shoulders as if a vise were being tightened.

I had read about this phenomenon and reread about it in honor of the occasion. According to Reichian theory (a type of psychology), our cultural pictures and our self-preserving pictures (my terms, not Reich's) show up in how we hold our body. (With that the Buddha would agree, as would any yoga instructor.) In my anger I had blown off the physical rigidity associated with the cultural and self-preserving picture of being a good and silent son. When I had apologized, I invited the tension back, and because for a few minutes I had been a free man, I now felt the tension as it returned. It took twenty years to change that phenomenon, and from time to time in moments of extraordinary "goodness," I can still feel my shoulders and neck tighten as my head feels squeezed.

In order to thwart my deepest urges, my self tries to get a grip on itself.

I was leading a workshop for young executives for a Fortune 500 company. During a small group session, one of the women was complaining about how overworked she was, and the other participants were attempting to provide her tactics for lowering the workload.

Without thinking it more than an obvious thing to do, I suggested to her that she go to her boss and say: "I am doing what I can. I can do no more."

She said that that was impossible. So I asked her what there was about her boss that was so off-putting. She said he was a good egg. Indeed, two or three of the group who knew him reassured her that he would be sad to think that he was overloading her.

"Well, then," I said, "you will go and tell him, will you not?"

She thought about it and then said, "No. I just can't do that."

"OK," I said, not yet realizing the depth of the issue, "at least say to us here in this group now, 'I am doing what I can. I can do no more.'"

She looked around the group for at least thirty seconds, took a deep breath, and burst into tears. "I can't do it," she wailed.

Five minutes later, when everyone was done clucking over her and hugging her and commiserating and she had regained control, I asked, "When you get back to your hotel room, will you look in the mirror and say: 'I am doing what I can. I can do no more.'"

She said: "I will try."

Her deepest response to her weariness of work was being prevented by a self-preserving picture derived from a cultural picture eons old of women who bore the babies, raised the children, did the laundry, cooked the meals, milked the cows, and fed the chickens without ever saying that they could do no more. No point telling her that she lived in a friendlier and less dangerous world where someone of her talents could decide that enough was enough. The picture of a belabored housewife working in the fields superseded the picture of the comfortable life for a talented executive.

The self and its pictures, the culture and its pictures are not friends to your deepest responses. While useful to ensure respect from your companions in life and to grease the social skids, they create the Creative Anxiety that prevents your living in *nirvana*. It is the gap between these pictures and your deepest feeling-responses that drives you into *samsara*. They warn you that your impulses toward freedom will ruin your life. For the most part that is a lie, but it is an effective lie, trapping you within the culture and your remembered past.

Not all Creative Anxiety is useful! Sometimes the gap between picture and reality must be closed by discarding or adjusting the picture.

Orientation

In the first three chapters, we established the need for a way of thinking about meditation that brought it into the layperson's world as a useful technique. The concern we were addressing was that the monastic model for meditation seemed to take away people's freedom, and we wanted to join the early Zen adapts and motorcycle riders exploring the possibilities of life. Creative Anxiety was presented as a model for what is going on internally that would allow us to be aware and seek freedom.

In the last chapter, we began the exploration of the imagining step of the model. How it both pulls us ahead with operational pictures, and limits our path for good and ill with cultural and self-preserving pictures. We will continue exploring each step in the upcoming chapters.

Buried in the middle of this chapter is an exercise that I am sure you will want to do. Or are doing. I am confident that you do not want this book to be simply interesting.

Chapter Five: Observing

Is There a You There?

We English-speaking people are accustomed to thinking of ourselves as a definite entity possessing certain capabilities. For instance, there is John, who has the capacity of observation, memory, imagination, feeling (the noun). I no longer think that way. As a Buddhist might, I think this way: There is observing, remembering, imagining, and feeling (the verb).

Whoops, there is no "John"!

I am alert enough to have noticed that in this moment there is a 240-pound body that most people call "John." And I have noticed that when observing, I am aware of an entity present that I think of as myself. So there is something there. But quantum physics and a well-taught Buddhist would say that what is there is a present and momentary action. Remembering my past actions leads me to think of myself as a noun, a permanent entity. But I am far from permanent. In the snap of the finger between now and a moment ago, I have changed mentally and physically. So I am a set of verbs, circling another verb, a body referred to as "John."

When observing, there rises a sense of this entity as it presently exists. When remembering, there rises a sense of this entity as it was. When imagining, there rises a sense of this entity as it could be. When feeling, there arises a sense of attraction or aversion to the present, past, or future. I desire it, or I desire something other than it to be the case.

It is impossible to clearly draw the line between the entity and its environment. When does food become "John?"? When he imagines eating it? When it is in the esophagus? The bloodstream? And when does it become waste? In the colon? The anus? The toilet bowl? (For a baby, flushing the toilet can be traumatic until he learns that excrement is no longer him.) When is a thought John's? When he sees it on the page? When he partially comprehends it? When he fully understands it? When he teaches it? And then how can he say he has this thought when it was and still is on a page? Is it not shared? So if two people are thinking the same thing, are they then one person? Of course not, but how separate are they?

It is a mess, and I cannot sort it out. I will simply hold the fact of the mess in the background. But out of the mess emerges for me a flowing reality, a world of interpenetrating verbs, to replace what I was taught as a child, a static reality, and a world of independent nouns.

I do know that observing is happening, and I am not at all sure about the entity that observes or the solidity of that which is observed. Just file that in the background. There are other books, one written by me, that explore this vigorously. I explain it a little here because you might notice my ambivalence about referring to "I." Sometimes I do, and sometimes I don't. It looks like I am here, but I am not sure that's the way it is.

The Queen of the Functions

"Observing" is the queen of the functions. All the other functions are blind until they are observed. The imagination runs on and on, responding to external kernels of stimulus and internal bumping of neurons and bodily urges without reflection on what it is doing until it is observed, and then based on aversion or attraction it seeks calmer and more orderly courses.

There is no intelligent aversion or attraction, no conscious intention, until observing begins, for it is observing that wakens the memory to past encounters with reality, to values learned at home or in school, to the realities of history. It is these value-laden memories that infect the imagining process and waken a feeling-response to move away from buying the new car tomorrow as the memory of the pile of present debt comes forward and the memory of daddy warning you of the consequences of being in hock and your history of five years digging yourself out of the last financial hole interfere with the flow that started with the back tires screeching and was now moving to the soft leather of the heated seats and your neighbor's envious smile.

"Observing" rules as a gentle queen. It brings not control but intelligence to the other functions. Or perhaps more simply, "observing" by reducing anxiety allows "remembering" and "feeling" to emerge, which coupled with "imagining" equals "intelligence."

Concepts Interfere with Pure Observation

"Observing" is neither simple nor easy. In the process of your growth, you collected many memories of that which you are about to observe. You have so many memories that with ease you can imagine the very thing you are supposed to be perceiving. That is what you almost automatically do.

Imagining is easier than observing. Past generations struggled to observe. Over two thousand years ago in the public parks of India, the monks gathered to simply sit and observe the body, feelings, thoughts, and phenomena. They had a hard time of it. Only a relative few reported awakening to the present reality. The Buddha's advice was to seek solitude somewhere other than a park. Even there something like a babbling stream might literally make a person crazy.

In our driven society, what are the odds you will observe the desk clerk, or your feelings about being in this hotel, or your mind racing with thoughts of tomorrow, or your body weary from hours in a pressurized cabin?

At the same time as you collected these memories, you collected feelings of aversion or attraction to them. Vast categories of past experiences waken feelings of desire or repugnance. You do not like women who wear boots. You are afraid of black men with dreadlocks. Denny's Restaurants are problematic. Anything that says "Mom" in the title makes you want it. Subarus are the cars of choice. You "need" a drink at the first sign of any bottle of alcohol.

Whatever the particular experience that dropped that memory into your system, the presence of something resembling that experience tends to bring not the reaction derived from the stimulus itself but the reaction derived from memory.

Instead of the woman before you, you see the result of a collection of women who you have known who wear boots, and you experience the image as that of a controlling shrew. Someone with different experiences seeing the woman in boots that he associates with women who play fast and loose delights in being in the presence of a highly available sex object. In the center of the storm is the actual woman who usually never wears boots but borrowed these from her roommate because her sneakers were muddy. But for good or ill, the odds are you will never meet this flesh and blood, particular, breathing woman. Indeed, as long as this process grinds on without interruption, you will meet no woman, or man, or tree, or cloud, or rain.

An Addition to the Practice

Observing is not easy. In the third chapter, I asked that you practice the Creative Anxiety process. In that practice you observe the other functions in the system as they occur. I would like you to add a moment on either end of the process.

Before observing the functions, take a moment to observe the breath. Pick a spot in your body, perhaps the diaphragm, or the nostrils, or the throat, and experience the breath as it moves in and out. Notice how the breath is in the foreground of your attention. In the background is the observing itself. Can you rest back into that observing? Perhaps yes, perhaps no.

Without judging yourself as to whether or not you could sink into the observing at this point, slide into the rest of the Creative Anxiety cycle. What is your imagination presenting to you? Are you drawn to it, or repelled by it? Can you experience the anxiety, the urge to act? Act.

Before moving on, in the brief moment of silence before you notice a new, real-life picture pulling you back to work or play, again see if you can rest back into simply observing without an object. And then slide back into your active life.

During the exercise, if the telephone or your computer rise in your imagination with a task that could be done with them, please skip on. As soon as you dial the phone or punch the mouse, observation will become difficult. Do something simple: Pick up a pen. Straighten a desk. Go to the toilet. Wash a dish. Pick up a diaper. It would be my hope that the day will come that you can automatically observe yourself having a phone conversation. But we are starting in an easier place.

The Creative Anxiety cycle brings your awareness to the process you are moving through. The pause before and after open you to your deepest being, that which is still there when there is no object.

The pause at the front of the cycle and the pause at the end might each last a minute. The cycle itself should take another three to five. Your obligation to learning is now five to seven minutes, several times a day. And at the same time you are still getting something done, and probably done better, and I suspect with more pleasure and relaxation. This is healthier than a cigarette break or a coffee break and cheaper.

Awareness of Being

In the pause before and after the cycle, we turn our attention to the observing itself. Can you be aware of the observing itself?

In the Creative Anxiety cycle, the function of observing views the other functions as objects. "Observing" observes "imagining," "feeling-response," "anxiety," "acting," and "bliss."

But can "observing" observe "observing"? The answer is: "Not exactly."

There is no way to look at whatever lies behind your eyes. However, you can be aware of the process of observing. It is not a looking at, but a sinking into.

There is richness here as the anxiety fades, the process gently moves forward, and all proceeds with a deep awareness. And in the field of that awareness, all else rises and fades.

Lovely.

For instance, I have just finished lunch, scrambled eggs and toast. I put some stuff away and washed out the frying pan in a dead, non-observing state. But then I noticed crumbs on the counter, and I woke up to the process. I observed the crumby counter and imagined it clean and felt the intention to clean it and cleaned it, and then the other counter and then the table. Right through the process, and then I stood there for a moment well aware of this process of awareness itself, observing crumbs, and images, and urges, and action, and now a pleasant contentment with life. As I said:

Lovely!

Besides All This

Observing multiplies freedom.

When I chose the title Creative Anxiety for this approach, I was focused primarily on assuring the reader that contemplating this way would not interfere with the creative process. But it does more than that; it enhances it.

First of all, where do the creative products of imagination come from? From combining what is in memory. And where do the contents of memory come from? Observation.

People who wish to write novels are encouraged to write down everything they possibly can of what they see. Someday they may pull from their notebook the twitches of the man at the next table and have their villain twitch similarly. The beard of the old man in the corner will reappear on the lawyer's chin. The waves plopping on the Wisconsin beach will be enlarged to California surf. The shy but determined look of the schoolgirl will reappear on the face of the new detective in the squad.

Everything you actually see can be added to the arsenal of what you can imagine, and everything that you do not see but is buried under other memories cannot be reclaimed for later use.

I listened to a children's author trying to explain to a group of would-be book writers that in order to describe climbing a mountain, she did not need to have had the actual experience; she simply enhanced the experience of climbing a hill, something she did almost daily. Question came upon question, indicating that the listeners had no idea what she was talking about, for after all a hill is a hill and a mountain a mountain.

After the lecture I slipped up to her and suggested that the problem might be that climbing is climbing, whether hill or mountain, but most people do not experience themselves while climbing an ordinary rise in the land so they cannot enlarge the gasping of the breath, the stress on the legs, the bent-over position, the pumping of the blood.

A children's author worth her salt experiences everything down to the last gnat. No matter how clever with words others are, the great story will come from the aware and observing person. You do not think that Hemingway ever caught a great fish miles from land and then fought sharks on the return, do you? But he had seen great fish and he had been far out to sea and he knew what a shark was like and he understood the beginnings of becoming old. All such awareness became fodder for his imagination and the epic *The Old Man and the Sea*.

I read the poetry of Mary Oliver and wonder if any other person besides she has ever really seen anything. Well, Deb Cooper has also. But she is a local poet, and you probably do not know her.

John Cowan

The Merits of Simply Seeing

Even in the present, simply seeing can seem to be the mark of extraordinary genius.

I was facilitating a human relations sensitivity group back in the sixties. During the first hour of our time together, Char, a sweet gray-haired woman in her fragile fifties, revealed to the other ten people her struggles at home with an alcoholic husband and young adult children showing every sign of following in his path.

She and the group were shocked when I turned to her after an hour of listening and said loudly, "Shut up!"

She not only became quiet but after three huge breaths burst into tears and then, knocking to one side the outstretched compassionate arms of her fellow participants, rushed out the door.

The group was to last another half-hour and did so with participants trying in several not so straightforward ways to tell me what a jerk I was and indicate that they too might leave this workshop forever. That, of course, worried me some.

After the coffee break we reassembled, and she was there thanking me profusely for preventing her from further spilling her guts to strangers before she had any reason to trust them. Others, too, once they understood her meaning, commented on my insight.

While I enjoyed the heck out of the praise, I did not want to be their sainted hero. I knew that today's enjoyment would be greatly marred by the confusion that would come later when I failed to live up to their ideals. So I told them the truth.

As the hour had progressed, more and more frequently she had interjected into her outpouring the sentence: "I wish somebody would tell me to 'shut up.'"

About the tenth time she said it, I noticed it, so after the fifteenth time she said it, I said it back to her. "Shut up!"

Observing and creativity are hooked in wonderful ways. As are observing and compassion.

One day I sat along the ship canal leading from the Duluth Harbor to Lake Superior. The canal is about a quarter-mile long, deep enough for oceangoing ships, perhaps a short city block wide, with a walkway on my side, and the walkway separated from the canal by a concrete railing. The cruise boat was leaving the harbor and had honked for the bridge, the bridge had sounded its bells and horn and lifted, fifty or so people gathered along the railing to watch the little ship go out. One family, mother and father and five children, walked beside the ship matching its pace, waving and shouting, and on the children's part jumping with excitement. That is, except the littlest, who could not see over the railing.

He tried to get his parents' attention, but they were engrossed in watching the cruise ship. His brothers and sisters were having their own small ecstasies and were unwilling to see what his problem was. He would run along and then stop to see if he could get a peek through the gaps in the wall, and then when that failed, he would try jumping again, and then the family would have left him and he would run to catch up and see if now they might pay attention, which they did not.

My heart broke for him. His parents cared not in the least. Were they disinterested because they lacked compassion for their own son? No, because they never saw what was happening.

Observation is the Queen, and without the Queen we are heartless indeed. And blind. And ineffective.

Our freedom is constrained to the few alternatives readily at hand, usually cultural and self-preserving pictures of possibility.

Exercise

From time to time, stop everything and be aware of your internal and external surroundings. The Buddha gives you four categories of things to be aware of: Your body, your feelings, your thoughts, and your surroundings. Then try moving slowly and staying in touch with all that. A thirty-second exercise.

Orientation

Having established the need for a model (a way of looking at what is going on) and laying out that model, we are now clicking our way through the steps of the model, or maybe I should be saying "aspects" since they do not occur in the same order every time.

We have considered two aspects (imagining and observing) and have two to go (anxiety and feeling/intention).

I will not bore you by reminding you of the importance of the tiny exercises.

Chapter Six:
Anxiety

Pathological Anxiety

In my seminary days, my eleventh year of study, third year of my postgraduate work, and twenty-third year of my life, I became deeply anxious. I could feel it in my forearms, which tended to tremble, and in my gut, which felt slightly sick almost all of the time. In my classes my mind constantly left the lecture subject and returned to my fear. Prayer was impossible except to pray that this fear would leave me. The only diversion from the fear was athletics, and even then as a hockey goalie when the action moved to the other end of the rink, my fear would return. (I was probably the only goalie in hockey who was only happy when people were shooting at him.)

I knew why I was afraid. The cold war was at its height, and I was afraid that the next plane I heard flying overhead was carrying the bomb that would start World War III. Those who lived through that era can attest this fear was not completely insane. There was a reasonable likelihood that such a bomb might fall and trigger Armageddon, but much less likelihood that it would be right over my seminary.

The gracious little campus was located on the flight path in and out of an international airport, which was also the home of navy fighter jets, so if I forgot for a moment that the war was on, the next plane over would remind me.

I struggled with this problem for several dreary winter months. Nothing helped. Not books. Not consultation with a spiritual advisor. Nothing. As spring arrived, I thought *If this does not stop, I am going to seek psychiatric help*. I would give it a couple more months, and then I would blow the whistle.

At the same time, I was happy to note that the diet I had begun the previous fall was successful. I had lost forty pounds, from about two hundred to one sixty. I could go off the diet and return to eating the bread and potatoes and desserts that I had not touched for the whole winter.

I stopped being anxious!

Within a couple of weeks after I came off the diet, the improvement was noticeable, and by the time I was leaving for summer vacation, a formation of navy jets would not interest me to the point of even looking up.

I never saw a medical professional about this, so I cannot speak with confidence, but something I read years later about starch in the diet makes me think that skipping all my starches left lots of little synapses uncoated and strumming their naked little hearts out for help. Absent a reason, the strumming sought and found World War III as a probable cause.

The first point of the story is that as well as anxiety arising from the imagined, anxiety creates its own threatening pictures. As I sat waiting for response from the motorcycle shop, I created several highly unlikely negative scenarios. Although they were unlikely, I thought them more likely than what actually happened: my tire was repaired in a reasonable time.

The second point is that in the seminary, my anxiety had little to do with war, or pictures, or anything psychological. It had to do with the absence of potatoes.

Your anxiety may be caused or influenced by neurological or chemical factors. I know nothing about this except my own suffering, and this book offers nothing to alleviate such problems. See your doctor.

I take this space for this topic and treat it this emphatically because I do not want anyone continuing to go through that hell because I have seduced them into thinking this practice will address that problem.

While I was not suicidal during my few months of anxiety, I certainly now understand why people commit suicide when faced with that implacable darkness year after year. If a chat with a professional psychologist might help, have the chat. If a pill will redress the balance, take the pill. I was lucky. All I needed was a potato.

Anxiety Blinds

The anxiety produced by the gap between the intended picture and the real, I have called "Creative Anxiety" to distinguish it from the kind cured by counseling or a pill. What is its effect upon awareness and observing and the rest of the Creative Anxiety cycle?

Why did not anyone else tell the sweet gray-haired lady to "shut up"? Granted that they might have chosen words that were less literal and politer in reflecting her own desires back to her, but still, why didn't they?

Because they were anxious, and anxiety, if too prevalent, blinds.

Imagine the experience of a fairly typical attendee. Barry has an advanced degree in psychology. He has been taught how to respond to the mentally ill in helpful ways. His work life is bounded with certain rules of conduct governing both him and his clients. They share with him their most intimate problems. He tells them nothing. They meet for fifty minutes, and no matter what the circumstance at the end of their meeting, it is over for the week.

His social life is predictable. Much of it with others like himself in training and occupation, and all of it softened by the realization on everyone's part that his background and his skills give him an advantage over others in interpersonal contact. He is respected and looked up to.

He has now registered for a strange workshop, something he has never experienced. The hotel desk clerk had given him a package of materials and told him to read the first page immediately. It said simply: "Tell no one anything about your background. Give them only your first name. Since we intend to focus on present behavior, share none of your history and ask for nobody else's history."

That certainly made him blink. He went through the first evening becoming increasingly uncomfortable, his comfort not assisted in the least by the casual dress and "unprofessional" behavior of the staff, who claimed they were here for their own growth and that would take precedence over working for his growth.

The next morning, when he checked into his sensitivity group for the first time, he found the facilitator in charge of the delicate operation of personal change toward more psychological health sitting on the floor with no more instruction to the assembling group than to say that it was up to the group to figure out a way to start. And then the facilitator tells someone to "shut up" without apology or explanation.

In summary, he has a nut for a leader, a bunch of unknowns for fellow searchers, he cannot let on who he is, and yet his internal picture of himself reinforced by years of study and successful work is that of a man who can help others. How does he make that image operational in this setting?

Is he anxious? Oh yes! Does he know he is anxious? No. Is he relieved when the old lady across the circle decides to spill her guts, take up airtime, and allow him to exercise his skill of seeming helpful? You're darn tooting! At last he can intend a picture that he can make happen.

And is there the slightest chance that with all that rolling around inside him, he will notice that the lady wants off the hook? Well, he didn't, so that makes the point.

Now if she were seeing him in his office where all the messages were that he was a professional doing his professionally authenticated thing, would he have been anxious? Not at all. I suspect that within ten minutes of her outpouring, he would have been asking himself, "What good is all this blabber doing?"

And the first time she said that she wished someone would tell her to "shut up," he would have intervened and said something like: "You are wondering if telling me all this is helpful."

And if she did not get that hint, he would have said later: "Let's explore if this is the best way for you to use this time."

Why didn't he?

Barry cannot close the gap between the picture he has of himself as a professional mental health worker and the reality unfolding in front of him and inside him because he is too anxious to think straight. He is not free to consider alternative pictures.

The World Is Obvious when Anxiety Is Absent

Barry told me a couple days later that Char had come to him and asked his opinion on her family problems. By this time completely devoid of anxiety, Barry looked her in the eyes and saw calmness there, an absence of anxiety, that begged for reality without the sugar coating, so he said, "While your family has its problems, I think the central problem is that you are a little crazy."

He reported (and she verified all this for me a day later) that she did not even blink. She said, "You're saying this as one friend to another?"

"No," he said, cheating on the workshop rules, "I am a mental health professional. I am saying this as a mental health professional."

She looked at him gravely, "I'll have to get back to you on this. This is a little disturbing."

Well, I guess it should have been disturbing. Here she was one moment the besieged rational center of a distressing family, and now a good friend (friendship came quickly in that setting) and a mental health professional was saying she and her craziness were the basic family problem.

From early afternoon until late evening, Barry worried about Char's reaction. He had said what he had said because he saw her calm centeredness, but it violated several of the rules of conduct he had been taught as a therapist. He was not living up to the old imagined picture. The gap between who he should be and who he was being created anxiety. Would she seek the privacy of her room to take an overdose? He could see it now. (His anxiety was creating its own pictures.)

But instead, as he sat by the pool, she pulled up a chair next to him. "That was very helpful," she said. "I am going home and tell my family what I have discovered. I am going to tell them that there is no help coming from me. I am crazy. They are going to have to figure this out for themselves. If they want to go to family therapy, I will come along, but I am going to make it clear to the therapist that I am not the solution. I am the problem. The children are young adults, and my husband is as old as I. They will have to be the solution. As for the rest of life, I may make a lousy mother, but everybody else finds my nuttiness charming. So send no one to fix me. I am going to be just fine as I am."

I am very happy that neither of them told me about this until it was over; my anxiety would have risen off the chart. But theirs did not, and a very difficult situation resolved itself marvelously.

Why did the parents not see the little boy jumping and peeking to see a cruise ship? They were anxious about their own experience. If they had paid attention to him, they might have missed something out there on the water.

Pictures and Anxiety

You see in this all the anxiety that occurred because of imagined pictures pulled from memory. The picture of the good therapist from his training raised Barry's anxiety, as he could figure no way to live up to it. Once he stopped living up to it, he performed very well indeed.

Char's picture of the good mother kept her anxious and struggling to save her family, and replacing it with a closer-to-reality portrait of the crazy lady allowed her to without anxiety declare herself the problem and get on with an otherwise happy life.

In last chapter's example, the parents probably had come to the canal drawn by a picture of their children seeing ships, but when the ship arrived, their picture of themselves seeing the boat was threatened by the agitation of their youngest child, and so in anxiety they ignored him and their original picture.

In all these situations, people were not free to follow their deepest impulses.

Observing and Anxiety

What to do when anxiety blocks you from proceeding?

Observe the anxiety, as it exists in your body. Here is a use for the preliminary exercise I offered in the last chapter. Focus on the breath. That will gradually calm you down. Then observe the rest of the body. Become aware of the tensions where they exist. Give them time to relax. This may get you room to think things through.

When I sat in front of my hotel room waiting for the news on my motorcycle with my anxiety driving me through the roof, I found that trying to be rational simply created more irrational pictures of possible outcomes. The shop would not have the tire. During the wobbling a part that lives only in Japan was broken. Their mechanics all have the flu and will be out for the rest of the month.

Observing the breath and then my body with its anxiety quieted me down to the point where I realized that I was stuck on a picture of the future that I need not be stuck on. But without that calming, my imagination would not have been free to begin spinning new and more achievable pictures.

Summary

In summary, there have been seven points made in this chapter so far:
1. The body can produce anxiety without the Creative Anxiety Process.
2. Anxiety itself produces frightening pictures.
3. The presence of an unachievable picture produces debilitating anxiety.
4. Anxiety blocks observing.
5. Anxiety blocks imagination.
6. The best way to begin to break the cycle is to observe the breath and the body.
7. Once a reasonable level of calmness is achieved, the next step is to imagine more achievable scenarios.

Impermanence

There is another source of creative anxiety. Most of us carry an image of ourselves as permanent. You expect that you will be alive forever. When somebody points out that you too are destined to die, you of course agree, but in your deepest heart you assume that you will live forever. But then there is the reality we must work with that we have this body that tends to fall apart.

Immense Creative Anxiety arises, for the picture and the reality are so different, so difficult a gap to bridge, so important an issue, and all of this presses down almost to the unconscious level.

This anxiety waits to bubble to the surface, but it only rises to view rarely, say at a funeral or when somebody in your office has a heart attack, or perhaps your car gets slammed into at an intersection and you walk away to sit on the curb while the paramedics diagnose you as in shock. ("Shock" often is a sudden reintroduction to reality.)

This anxiety also bubbles just below the surface, interfering with all other emotions and all other thoughts. It is an existential anxiety. A fear of not being. Deeper and more powerful than any other fear.

Cures for existential anxiety are plentiful and varied, starting with whisky to dull the fear for the evening and then later in life for the afternoon and then finally from breakfast on.

Religion has its solutions. The great religions of the world offer such solutions as reincarnation with the possibility of continuing on as a different entity at a later time, and the possibility of resurrecting in a new body and in a new heaven. The Buddha and Jesus of Nazareth, contrary to their own disciples, ignored the question of afterlife, focusing instead on happiness now.

I have nothing to add. I know I am impermanent, and in this case I think that to reduce my anxiety, there is nothing to do but cease imagining myself as permanent and allow the image to dissolve to that of a happy and pain free death whenever the universe sends it.

I mention this topic here because far from being idle religious speculation, comfort with the appearance of impermanence is central to your freedom from anxiety at a deep level, and any attempt to influence anxiety at the level of the Creative Anxiety model must take into account that a picture of myself as permanent will cause me deep anxiety unless in some way I have addressed the gap between that and what most obviously happens to the human body.

Ignoring the problem will not make it go away.

Orientation

Our premise is that you do not need to sit still to wake up to reality. All you have to do in order to be awake in motion is to continue to observe your functioning in motion. While sitting still, the Buddha recommended that you observe your body, feelings, thoughts, and phenomena. We are now exploring what happens when we move. Knowing what happens in general makes it easier to observe what is happening in a specific instance. First I introduced you to the Creative Anxiety model as a general description of what you might observe, and now we are walking through each step of the model to understand it more deeply. We have finished studying imagining, observing, and the rising of anxiety, and now we will look at the process of intending.

As we proceed, note how cultural and self-preserving pictures limit our freedom to act from our deepest impulses in response to an immediate situation, as indeed sometimes our long-range operational pictures do.

The Third Parable:
The Motorcycle Club

Once there was a motorcycle club where everybody liked everybody immensely. So for their motorcycle trips, they always rented a school bus.

Chapter Seven: Feeling-Response and Intention

Valuing Feelings

A meditation practice that denigrates feelings may lead to a blissful understanding of something, but it leads to a blissful understanding of something not quite human. For this practice, Creative Anxiety, we will be deeply aware of these feelings, hold them in great respect, but manage them so that we can move toward our images of the future without fear.

Feelings are a component part of the human being. Every stimulus is worthy of a reaction, and every stimulus creates at least a rudimentary response. However, we would go quite mad if we responded to everything. So we develop the habit of ignoring our feelings. But the more we ignore the feelings, the more we shrink as human beings. And the more we allow the feelings to rise until they provoke response and intention, the more we become deeply and powerfully human. Free in our imagining. Free in our choices. Free in our actions.

You and I do not intend to wimp out. We intend to become tiger slayers. The puppet who takes off her strings is not our God, but our model.

A Reminder of the Cycle from Stimulus to Feeling to Intention

In this model, a stimulus provokes a picture of what could be. You are attracted or repelled by the picture. In the broadest terms, you form an intention to move toward the picture or to move away from it. Once the intention is formed, immediately anxiety rises about the distance between reality and the picture. You swing into action to reduce the anxiety.

Differences from Ordinary Meditation

In books on ordinary meditation practice, "intention" is not explored beyond the intention to attain enlightenment and the intention to behave in ways likely to provoke enlightenment. Since the desired meditative state is not a state of motion, even the intention to be enlightened is viewed as suspect. The desired state is a state of completion, contentment with what is. "Intending" implies some imperfection in the present moment. If I am "intending," I cannot be experiencing completion or contentment.

To the contrary, "intending" does not bring on the imperfection of the present moment, but the level of anxiety this intending is producing creates *samsara*. A certain level of creative anxiety is tolerable and helpful, but some levels of creative anxiety block awareness. Being a little afraid works just fine. Too much afraid, and your eyes are blinded.

As I stood by the motorcycle in the rest stop just before the Mackinac Bridge, having just set aside my picture of crossing the bridge with its corresponding intention, I experienced completion and contentment. But moments later, as I crossed the Mackinac bridge intending to reach the far side, despite the fact that I was in motion and incomplete, short of an objective, with an unrealized picture of success, I still experienced deep happiness and contentment.

According to most meditation texts, my midway state should have produced the discontentment that smudges *nirvana* (the state of happiness) and makes me see *samsara* (the state of discontent). But it did not. In the midst of creating, between reality and the picture of a better state, while motivated by creative anxiety, I can still be free from debilitating fear, awake, enlightened, living in the kingdom of light.

Indeed, that midway state is often the best lighted of my moments. With two outs in the inning and a runner on second, as I stood by the third base bag, the batter smashed a line drive to my left. The ball went like a rocket. He hit it while it was two feet off the ground, and in a blink it shot across the infield, never varying from that height. At one and the same time, I fell to my left, drove with both feet, launched myself into a full stretch, my gloved hand extended as far as it could be stretched. The ball buried itself in my glove. I hit the ground, rolled to my feet, dribbled the ball toward the pitcher's rubber, and began walking to the bench. The batter had just made his first step to first and had not yet released his bat.

I have nearly perfect memories of the moment of incompletion, the ball two-thirds of the way on its path, my body in midair. I can see the pitcher turning to follow the ball, the shortstop with his glove half-raised, the ball slowly moving back and forth as it creased the air with its flight (it was not spinning). The event occurred forty-eight years ago, and I remember it so well because it was a moment of unusual brightness and clarity. (It was a moment of unusual athleticism also. This was an intramural "B" league game. I don't want you to get a false impression of my skills. However, I was a very good hockey goalie, so catching line drives was not an unfamiliar occurrence.)

If to live in light I must not intend anything, how could I have experienced such brightness in this moment when I intended most sincerely to do something most difficult?

Indeed, how could Jesus live in the kingdom of God while he was teaching? How could the Buddha claim that he was awake while crossing a field?

Acting without Dysfunctional Anxiety

Intention creates anxiety, and anxiety creates action. For you to experience the moment free and awake, anxiety cannot rise to the point where it blocks observing.

This is the answer to the questions raised by the story in the first parable, The Heart of a Tiger. When the monk, instead of freezing or running for his life, took a bamboo pole, created a spear, and drove it through the heart of the tiger, he had to forget his fear. He would have encountered less risk if he had ducked into the crowd. To paraphrase an old joke, for safety he did not have to outrun the tiger, just one of the ninety-nine other monks.

When he forgot his fear and acted, he discovered what it meant to be deeply human. Intention flowed into action without the confusion of self-preserving pictures. Indeed, if fear had intervened, there would have been no intention and no action except that of leaving the scene and abandoning the other monks (whose fear was about to get at least one of them killed).

In terms of our model, the other monks clung so tightly to the picture of their own safety that they were prepared to run. (However, as is normal for humans, they were paralyzed from any action, probably because they were waiting to find out what everyone else thought the appropriate action to be.) Because of his deep realization that to be human was to be concerned for everybody (but not to wait for everybody to tell him what needed doing), the picture that emerged for him, which created an attractive and intended possibility, was of him killing the tiger.

He was free. They were trapped. He could choose to run or fight. They could choose only to run, or freeze.

How was it that I who played B league intramural ball had a moment of looking like a major league third baseman? Everything happened too quickly for my anxiety to rise to the debilitating level. I who have muffed slow grounders and dropped pop flies because as I waited for them to arrive, my fear of being exposed as a failure turned my limbs to lead, startled by the power of the line drive, instantly intended to catch it and dove without fear. I not only caught the ball but saw the world clearly in the process. My body was free to do what it wanted to do without the limiting effects of picturing failure.

Anxiety will also rise when competing pictures of the future struggle for your attention. Yesterday while talking to a friend of mine about his involvement in this very book, I noticed his eyeballs beginning to flicker. We were at a critical spot in the conversation, discussing his gathering a group of his friends to become testers of the product, see if it worked. I knew he was fascinated and eager to pull this off, yet his eyeballs were twitching.

It turned out that he was overdue to meet his wife. Two competing pictures, and the anxiety begins to rise to the debilitating level, even to the eyeball level.

Take a second. How many competing pictures are pulling on you right at this moment? Granted, I hope, that this book is the center of your focus, but what is there just beyond the margins of your awareness tugging for your attention? As they come into view, if they are of any worth, your creative anxiety will begin to rise, for all of them cannot be done at once.

Examples of Action without Fear

On the television news you will often hear people interviewed who are denying that they are heroes despite the fact that everyone else including the reporter are insisting that they are. "I just acted," they say. "I saw the boat capsize, so I jumped into the water, swam twenty yards, and pulled the child to safety. Anybody would have done it."

Well, not exactly. In the instant the boat capsized and the child hit the water, this hero saw two or three possibilities, and he selected the picture of the child being saved; he had a feeling-response to it, which response was to jump in. That became his intention and, bang; he hit the front page as a hero.

But surely among the possibilities he saw was the possibility of he himself drowning. If he did, he immediately dismissed it as unimportant. If he had seen it as critical, he would have known that jumping in risked it happening, and he would have stayed ashore.

When I was a young parish priest, Mrs. Olsen, a parishioner of ours, had congestive heart failure. Since she was very poor, she lived in a tiny basement apartment a block away. She joked that the local fire station was filled with her buddies since every two or three weeks they came to her house and carted her off to the county hospital. One of my jobs in life was to visit her.

I hated it.

First of all, she was not very interesting. Basement life would placid out the brightest of people, and she was not very bright. (When in the seminary I pictured myself helping the poor, I saw myself helping very bright and appreciative people. In real life, I found most of my poor were a wee slow and very demanding.)

Second, she kept having heart attacks, and I did not want to be the person who responded too slowly and let her die. My anxiety when with her was off the charts. Every time she moved, I thought this was the movement that would end her life. I endured other dull and more demanding people. She was the only one of our poor I ducked from.

On one of my days off, my car loaded with a canoe and my fishing gear in the backseat, I passed her apartment, thanking God that visiting was not my obligation this day although I had put her off now for a couple of weeks. And then, without thinking, I pulled over, turned off the car, and headed in for an hour's visit.

Lovely. A bright hour. You know why?

I had decided that I did not need to protect my picture of myself able to handle all conditions gracefully, and could risk looking stupid as the local firefighters hauled her dead body out the door. My fear dropped, and my picture of her happiness when I would arrive took over. And even beyond that, my picture of what a good priest should do that had hovered over my head for the last two weeks was finally allowed precedence.

Instead of being tugged and pulled by competing pictures, I now had a clear intention.

Intention Is Me

There was another factor in my joy in being in Mrs. Olsen's apartment. I was doing something most of the forces impinging on me in that moment did not want me to do.

Boethius in the fourth century defined "person" as the center of attribution of a rational nature. Without diving too deeply into Aristotelian metaphysics, or perhaps psychology, he is saying that when you answer the question "Who is responsible for this?" that "who" is a person.

At the same time, if my actions result in any given instance simply from the sum of coinciding forces, then in that moment I am not a person. And in the moments when I observe the forces and decide what direction to take, I am then a person.

My experience is that when I calmly intend even the most minor of events, my life immediately brightens. It is unintentional habits, or unintentional responses to cultural patterns, or unintentional commitments to distant pictures, or unintentional actions to continue to present to the world the same person who was here yesterday and the day before, that put me to sleep.

A Small Exercise

The intent of this exercise is to experience the rise and fall of the feeling-response until it closes on a single picture and becomes an intention.
1. Sit quietly for a moment, focus on your breath; get yourself prepared for observing the experiment.

2. Think of something you could do, and allow yourself to begin to feel and respond to it. Write down a couple of words as a title for it. Do nothing.
3. Think of something else you could do, and allow yourself to begin to feel and respond to it. Again, make a note to refer to. Do nothing.
4. Think of something else you could do, and allow yourself to begin to feel and respond to it. Write a third note on the page. Do nothing.
5. Now begin to review the alternatives simply by allowing your attention to move from one note to another to another. Until one rises from the others demanding action. Wait for the intention to settle in and the anxiety to act on the intention to rise. Do it.

Are you awake? This exercise wakes me up every time.

Orientation

I will not insult you by mentioning the need to do the exercises, especially the one just above.

We have been examining each function, or step, or aspect of the Creative Anxiety model, which we have put into place to give us a way of observing ourselves in action. We are done with that. The next chapter will pull together some practical advice on how to use the model to be awake and working at the same time.

Chapter Eight:
Creative Anxiety

Strategic Pictures of Success

The hoped-for outcome of reading this book is a layperson's life of freedom and choice and action coupled with awareness and brightness. That means the life of one who keeps the world functioning, not the life of a monk or hermit. Moderate success in the world will be important. You must allow clear and specific strategic pictures of success to emerge.

1. Draw these pictures with clear and sharp lines. Not the West Coast someday, but Vancouver Island in June. Not a kindly personality vaguely employed, but specific kind acts toward specific people. Clear pictures draw energy and activity without needing the force of willpower. You will not move toward the good because you have determined to, a painful, grunting, and futile process, but because the good draws you, a fluid and lightsome process.
2. Draw these strategic pictures in all areas of your life. This is not just about operational pictures; also visit the world of cultural and self-preserving pictures. You need not be their slave. Some you can select and enhance because they genuinely appeal to you. Some you can remove because

you have no taste for them. The culture gave me an ideal picture of the hardworking person. For most of my life it has served me well, and I left it on my wall of strategic pictures. Now that I am old, it is not helpful. What is a seventy-three-year-old man doing driving himself to produce? I know the picture of the hardworking hero makes me miserable, and that awareness is gradually loosening the tape that holds it in its privileged position.
3. Ten such strategic pictures would be about the right number. About fifteen years ago, my wife conducted an exercise in a group, and I played along. Given a dozen magazines, we were to cut out pictures that portrayed who we hoped to become and what we hoped to accomplish. I cut out nine pictures, two of which have not been useful; five have been for the most part fulfilled, and two have not yet been given time to ripen and maybe never will. But the pictures, casually created, have indeed given me direction, and still hang on my wall, behind me and to the left.

Once these strategic pictures are firmly implanted in your memory, they will influence your imagination to select what you are doing in the short term.

The rule will be: Allow your feeling-responses to flow toward these strategic pictures, creating intentions and actions as the spirit moves you.

Anxiety

The difference between your pictures and the reality will produce Creative Anxiety. It is this anxiety that induces work. Unlike many meditation practices that deplore any anxiety, this practice encourages enough creative anxiety to keep the motors running, but not enough to interfere with the ability to see the world as it is and to respond to it with feelings other than anxiety.

Four things you can do to manage creative anxiety:

1. Pay attention to the level of your anxiety and its causes. Simple awareness helps.
2. Work is a healthy response to creative anxiety. You may be normally anxious to fulfill the promise of an interesting picture. Get to work on it, and the anxiety will drop.
3. If you find that you are working frantically without joy or hope in picture fulfillment, recognize that the work wheel has spun out of control. You may have set for yourself a hopeless goal. You may be caught up in the work syndrome of the culture. You may be pulled among competing pictures. Review your pictures. Adjust your situation.
4. If the situation above persists, this may not be creative anxiety that you are experiencing. It may be chemically induced. You may need a doctor. If so, go see one.

The rule will be: Be aware of and responsive to your level of anxiety. Adjust your pictures of the future to adjust your Creative Anxiety.

Managing Constraining Pictures

Pictures can limit your freedom. This usually occurs when:
1. With limited awareness you are intending a useless cultural or self-preserving picture. Anxiety rises as it constrains your ability to pursue what you would prefer. You are trapped. Observe the picture, and it will lose its grip.
2. You are intending an operational picture that is too distant for immediate work and therefore life becomes dull. Select a closer picture on the path to it and intend it. Distant pictures turn you off. Even if the intention is to save your city. Immediate pictures turn you on. Even if the intention is to press down on the toaster switch.

Clinging

In the Buddha's system, there are four noble truths: 1) the fact of suffering; 2) the cause of suffering, clinging; 3) the cure for suffering, cease clinging; and 4) the prescription, The Eightfold Path, starting with the realization that nothing is permanent.

In the Creative Anxiety model, anxiety can be quieted and life become joyful by holding a picture without clinging to it. Imagine the future held in your clenched hand. Then imagine the future resting in your open hand.

Like a small bird, if you grasp it, it will struggle for freedom and either escape or die in your hand. In your open hand, it may indeed fly away if that is what it must do, but if it does not, for the moment you possess it in all its glory. So it is with the future.

Awareness

There is a cycle within the cycle that leads to the joy of being awake. As you observe and adjust your pictures, your anxiety will drop. As your anxiety lowers, your ability to see increases. The pictures of what you want to do and what you want to be sharpen and become more reasonable.

After years of missing the wastebasket with anything I threw at it, I now hit bull's-eyes ninety percent of the time. I thought at first that this meditation practice makes me more accurate. But then I observed and noted I now moved several steps closer to the basket before I threw the object. I have become more aware of what is possible.

Pictures awaken your feeling-responses, turning them into intentions. As you work, your anxiety drops. Life becomes a free-flowing dance of this possibility reached for and seized and savored as the next possibility rises into awareness.

Your existence becomes bright and joyous as a hawk rising on spring thermals. And you become a bright star for others. Your interactions, too, take on this lightsome quality, for the presence of others stimulates your imagination to see operational possibilities in common tasks and pleasant possibilities in the shared relationship. Defenses lower as your mind and heart play with other minds and hearts.

Some of my happiest moments were with the engineers of Honeywell Aerospace, all fearlessly confronting a common problem and sharing ideas freely. Joy amidst crew cuts and slide rules.

The Interpersonal

Parties are difficult. People come at you quickly and immerse you in interpersonal demands. There is little time to allow the fullness of the other person to be observed and the imagination to produce a deep response to who they are. So cultural and self-preserving pictures emerge. "How do I survive this without irritating others and still hold together the image of myself that I have chosen to present to the world?" becomes the only question.

I admit I usually avoid any but the "six people at a table for four hours" version of a party for that very reason. Some one of the Christian saints once said he never left his room that he did not return a worse man. That is strong, but still when I am forgiving myself my suffering, it is helpful to know I am not the first so to be confounded.

Bottom-line because of the power with which they approach you, people encounters need to be managed. And when they cannot be? Give up gracefully. Sometimes freedom is not available. Enjoy what is.

Confliction

If you feel locked in tension, you may be pursuing conflicting goals. My father was a union president, a man in pursuit of justice, and at the same time a man who liked to be liked, a raconteur, and the guy on the block who knew your name and lighted up when he saw you. Often these two pictures of what he wanted out of life coincided; he was pursuing justice for the sake of his friends. But sometimes they did not, as when he sold out his own department's five-cent-an-hour raise in favor of an increase from two cents to three for everyone in the company.

Living with this type of conflict cost him an ulcer by the time he was fifty and probably helped him become an alcoholic a few years later. I have the same conflict, and my only learning from his experience was how to avoid the alcohol and the ulcer. My advice to you who also find such conflicts is that knowing they are there helps greatly, but does not resolve the tension.

In this case, remembering that clinging is the cause of suffering is the cure. One or both of your pictures may have to be the bird held loosely in the hand that is allowed to fly away if it must.

When feeling trapped and seeking freedom, the first question must be "What am I holding onto that is trapping me?"

Anger

Our emotions have their uses. When faced with the difficult, anger can be helpful in lifting our energy and strength to the point where we can do what needs to be done. On the other hand, anger can be a nuisance, poisoning the atmosphere, making good work and joy impossible.

When you feel the flash of anger, check to see which of your pictures of what should happen are being violated. In some instances, your anger will be justified and useful. In others, it will be counterproductive.

As I step out on the porch, I feel anger. The paper delivery person has tossed the paper around the corner, where I will need ten cold steps to get it. She has violated my picture of what should be. How important is it that this picture be actualized? Next to zero. I forget it, and the anger subsides.

I see a child being verbally abused in the supermarket by her mother. My anger rises. My picture of how children should be treated is being violated. Before I make a move, I review some alternative pictures of what my anger will bring about. Will my anger do any good? Angry parent confronted by angry bystander? Probably not useful. Perhaps I can find some sly and not angry approach that will at least cause this moment to be over. (One expert recommends first commiserating quickly with the parent on the difficulty of raising children and then without waiting for a response asking the parent for directions to the hardware store.)

My daughter has been attacked on a college campus. The administration says that it will look into it, with that tone of voice that indicates it is not of much importance to them. I feel my anger rising. I say, "Since this seems unimportant to you, you will hear from our lawyer. I plan to sue you for not protecting my daughter on your grounds." And I will let my anger carry me forward in service to my picture of my daughter's and her friends' safety without blushing about how not so nice I am being.

Daydreaming and Other Mind Games

Some pictures are too distant for real work. They attract the imagination to play with them by daydreaming and compulsive planning. There is no harm in this in itself. It is even somewhat useful to review various scenarios of how something might be accomplished and quite motivating to see oneself doing the possible, and it is at least entertaining to dream of doing the impossible.

Over the winter, I mentally set up camp at various sites I plan to visit in the summer. I think through what I will bring, how I will pack the bike, what tools are no longer useful, what sleeping gear needs to be improved, which routes combine the efficient and the pleasant. And from time to time, a new idea or approach occurs. I see myself pulling in to Lake George and being welcomed by people I have only known on the Internet. The more often I do this mentally, the more likely it is that next summer I will actually arrive in New York.

And at times I visualize myself as the closer in the final game of the World Series. What the heck, who is hurt by this as long as I do not convince myself to show up at a major league camp for spring training?

So really no harm done. I have had a vacation from life. However, a bit of life has slid by without my living it, and that is at least a tad unfortunate. Which brings us to "the here and now."

The Here and Now

Another way of characterizing life in the kingdom of light is to say that it is life in the here and now. Instead of mind games that take me to a distant place and time, I can be present to this moment and this place.

When you want to return to where in actuality you are, check what picture is in your mind. It is a distant picture; otherwise, you would be here, not wherever there is.

To enter the here and now, replace that picture with a closer one: I will make a cup of coffee. I will type a page of my book. I will take out the garbage. It makes no difference what the picture is, just that it can be approached immediately.

Let us say you queue up coffee making. With that before you, head for the kitchen. Now queue up taking the pot down. Before moving, let's turn it into smaller operations. Find it. Reach for it. Grasp it. Lower it.

By now life should be feeling bright and relaxed. Hang in there through the entire coffee making process, and you may be good to go without this much concentration for a while. With some practice, living in the light becomes more ordinary and less unusual.

While I was waiting for the repair of the flat tire, I began clutching a picture of myself on time at home. This was an impossible picture to fulfill, one causing suffering and keeping me from the present. I could have replaced it with a picture of my harassing the service manager into compliance with my desires. That would have brought me into the here and now and brought brightness, but not success, since there was little he would be likely to do to speed the process. The picture of buying and reading a cheap novel brought me into the here and now and kept me there, because it gave me a picture that could be fulfilled now.

The rule of thumb is that if you are not living in brightness, you are focusing on a picture that is too distant and it is pulling you out of focus on the immediate.

Judging

Being aware of your feeling-response to stimuli is critical to being free and alive. That is not the same as deciding if things are good or bad. I have avoided many situations and many possibilities that I could have thought were good. Others thought them good. And I have been in several that I found attractive, but others thought them best avoided. (I played goalie in hockey in the days when we did not wear masks. I loved it to the point when there were pickup games I would get my pads and play in the nets of the weaker team. Few sought my job. Two other than myself, as I recall, thought "goalie" equaled "good." About fifty skaters thought it equaled "bad.")

Take life without judgment. Some great person said that you should be kind to others because each of us is engaged in a great battle. The man banging his head on the wall may be doing it to silence the voice telling him to buy a machinegun and slaughter everyone on the village square. She may dress like a slut because nobody has ever loved her really. He may be cold and arrogant because he is sad and frightened.

You do not know what is going on inside others. Maybe you do not want to be around these three. You feel aversion. So, fine. But do not judge them. The act of judgment takes you out of the immediate world and places you in a make-believe world that is just not much fun.

Not only judging people, but judging cars, and dogs, and lawns, and polar bears. Be attracted, be repelled, but do not judge. It screws you up.

The act of judging introduces into the field of the here-and-now response a scorecard, a cultural picture that interferes with the straightforward response to present reality. You are no longer responding to what is happening but to a concept of what should happen. Jesus in the gospels shows such openness to sinners because he is responding to who they are right now, not who they are when compared to the way people should be. He only gets really annoyed with people who are trying too hard to live up to a standard and in the process are being jerks.

The Past

I construct myself by looking at my past actions and thinking that in sum they make me. Try ignoring your past. Try seeing the past as a long tail attached to your bottom that you are forced to drag through the rest of your life. Then imagine yourself cutting it off. I regularly go to a coffee shop where I have identified myself as "Emil," my grandfather's name. (Pronounced long "a" then "mill" in case you and I bump into each other there.)

This ruse helps me forget this "John" guy whose long and quite important past I am dragging through the rest of my life. And lets this amnesiac Emil have a quiet cup of coffee. Unfortunately after three years the staff now knows Emil, and also the fact that they are to make a twelve-ounce soy latte in a bowl to make him happy. So now I too remember Emil and try to be consistent with his past actions. Emil is developing a tail and becoming a person.

On the occasions I chop off the tail, only the now is real, a much happier state. Hawks don't fly with thirty-foot tails.

On Being Asleep

Many people, perhaps most people, are asleep. There is nothing you can do about that.

Jesus tells the parable of the man who found a treasure in the field, so he hid it again, sold everything he had, and bought the field. Since by law the treasure would not be his for fourteen years, he now had nothing to live on and could not even show others the treasure lest he be turned in to the authorities. All he had was the treasure.

Unfortunately that is the life of the mystic, even the motorcycle mystic. All other pleasures come a distant second to living in the light, and there are very few people who know what you are talking about when you live in the light. So it is a lonely hobby. To be deeply alive is an adventure to which few want to commit.

Both Jesus and the Buddha say that this is not the life for those who want to be tightly connected to others. Jesus said you had to cut your family ties, and the Buddha said you had to kill your parents. As you struggle to live in the light, others, with the comprehensiveness of a fog, will quietly darken your days with their incapacity to understand.

It makes life a little like a motorcycle journey. You meet people on the way, but you do not hang together very long. The likelihood that you are going to the same destination with the same interim stops is low.

A phenomenon I consider quite odd is the groupieness of some motorcycle riders. After spending great amounts of money to ride a machine that gives them individual freedom, they then clump together and ride down the road in groups of six or ten or sometimes hundreds. This, of course, blocks almost absolutely their freedom to respond to stimuli, develop new pictures, and swerve that volatile little machine off of one road and onto another.

At least in a car, you can argue with the other people in the car, but in this herd-like stampede, you are trapped until the next stopping point from even saying that you saw a white buffalo in the field and would like to take a picture.

Even groups dedicated to pursuing the mystical are suspect. They function with the understanding of the least perceptive member.

You and I, we must ride these motorcycles alone if we hope to ride in the kingdom of light, but perhaps with this book, we have at least met.

Intention Is Me

Whenever you are asleep and would wake up, simply do something intentionally. Turn off the television or decide that you really want it on. Decide to sweep up the crumbs. Decide not to sweep up the crumbs. Decide to say nothing for the next ten minutes.

I found fasting for days made me feel immensely strong. I had decided against the most fundamental pressure of self-preservation not to do the most ordinary of things: eat. I found continuing to run when tired alerted me to this magnificent being that I am that can keep a body running that wants to quit. And I find that continuing to sit at this keyboard when my body claims that it needs to go to the toilet creates alertness in me and beauty around me.

All this is because for this brief moment I am other than all the forces pressing on me.

Is This the Last Word?

With some boldness I have referred to the results of Creative Anxiety as living in the kingdom of light, as *nirvana,* as enlightenment, and as bliss. Perhaps by now, if you have been trying this as you go, you too can attest to the fact that it does create quite a different set of sensations than the ordinary, a deeper contentment, a peace even while in the midst of turmoil.

But is this all there is? Earlier I asked you to take a moment at the beginning and the end of each exercise to be aware of awareness itself. This is a doorway to deeper realization.

As you move through life using the Creative Anxiety process, your attention is on the foreground, on yourself acting. We have tried to allow that to be an intentional and aware process. But underneath it lies the background. "Existing." If you can drop into awareness of it during moments of inactivity, a door may swing open to infinity.

This trail has been described in many other books, my own *Taking Jesus Seriously: Buddhist Meditation for Christians* among them. *Creative Anxiety* is intended to stretch the practice described in such books into the world of action, but not to supplant what they might teach you.

So this is not the last word, nor do I think there ever should be a declaration of the last word. Someone very soon will undoubtedly improve on this book. But hold off for a couple of years, will you? I too am a layperson in the world, and the royalties from this are part of my long-range operational picture.

Orientation

Has this been a long and somewhat bumpy ride? In some ways, I am feeling much as I do after I cross Montana and the Dakotas on US2. Windbeaten and seat sore. A short recap might be useful.

The starting point was the feeling that normal meditation has a killing effect on the energy to attack life and live in freedom. In search of an antidote to the crash-and-burn world of everyday existence that would still have the merit of deepening awareness, I introduced the thought that we might meditate on the creative process we used while moving through life.

I suggested that in the course of meditating on that, you would find aspects of that process that produced more freedom in your life and aspects that constrained that freedom. In becoming aware of what the process was doing, you would find that the process would work more smoothly and more effectively and you would become a freer person.

So now I suggest that you go through life observing yourself creating short-term operational pictures and fulfilling them. That you set long-term operational pictures, but that you be careful to hold them loosely or they will steal freedom from your present moment. And that you study carefully the cultural and self-preserving pictures locked into your imagination because, while sometimes necessary, they are a constant constraint on your freedom.

The paragraphs above were a little like pitching camp and looking around to see where I have been and where I might be going. But first, a cup of tea. But first find the stove. But next, let us assemble it. Screw the top on the red can, oh what a glorious day it is becoming. Who cares if the book is published? Who cares if it fits the needs of the meditating community? Who cares if I am seen as one smart fellow?

Let me carry the water bag to the pump. Radiance.

The Last Parable: The Hawk and the Fox

For the thirteenth time this month, after an hour spent stalking a rabbit, the fox, a leap and three bounds from his lunch, felt the shadow of wings, saw the clump of feathers descend on prey, and mourned the disappearance of rabbit and the neighborhood hawk back into the air. "Enough," she said.

The next morning she strolled by the hawk's favorite branch. There he sat, looking quite fed and satisfied. After exchanging pleasantries, she asked him what kind of hawk he was: Red, Sharp-Shinned, Coopers?

"Why," he said, "I have never given it much thought. What good would it do to know what kind of hawk I am?"

"Well, how are you to tell if you are a low-flying hawk or a high-flying hawk? How will you know if you build big nests or small? How will you know if you prefer rabbits or mice? Do you prefer to attack from the front or the back? Or perhaps the side?"

"My, that is a lot to think about," said the hawk, and being a fundamentally industrious sort, he began to think about all this most thoroughly. First he went online and researched hawks. And then he began to work from his own proclivities toward what kind of hawk he might be, and then when he had that type isolated, he tried to work back from the picture on the page to what he looked like and what he liked to do. Time after time he would nearly have the problem solved, and then something would turn up that proved he was not the type of hawk he thought he was.

Two weeks passed. Since he was studying, he had no time for foraging, and he had grown quite frail. He noted the fox standing below, plump and healthy. Two hawkless weeks of eating rabbit had proven quite satisfying. "How is it coming?" asked the fox. "Any answers yet?"

"None yet," said the hawk weakly, "but I am still searching. By the way, how did you ever discover what kind of fox you were?"

"Oh, I have no idea," said the fox, "never gave it much thought. Mostly I just think about lunch."

"You mean you have wasted your life thinking about 'rabbit'?"

"Well usually, yes indeed," said the fox, carefully observing the hawk as he wobbled unsteadily on his perch, "but recently I have begun to consider the possibility of 'hawk.'"

Summary of the Creative Anxiety Process

1) The first function is "observing." I am capable of being aware of what is happening in my body, my feelings, my thoughts, and the world around me. So I observe, and I appreciate what is.
2) As an adult, I have memories. I am able to combine these memories in various ways to construct possible futures. This function I call "imagining." I also refer to it as "picturing."
3) When I use my imagining to construct possible futures, the most attractive of these pictures will cause me to desire to make it real. The ability to desire a particular outcome is one of my functions. I refer to this function as "feeling-response." I am attracted to or repelled by the imagined image. This is at one and the same time a feeling and a response. When it rises to the point to provoke action, it is called an "intention."
4) As soon as I have decided that a future is one that I want to make real, as soon as I have an intention, I experience "anxiety" because until I do make it real, I have failed. The level of this anxiety varies depending on the importance to me of the outcome and the difficulty of the path to the outcome. I refer to this anxiety as "creative anxiety" to distinguish it from pathological anxiety.

5) This creative anxiety drives me to work to close the gap between my ideal future and my present reality. The greater the anxiety, the greater I am driven. I am "acting."
6) To the extent I am able to observe this process at work, to that extent the functions in the process will organize themselves to produce the future with minimal creative anxiety.
7) To the extent that I live without anxiety, even creative anxiety, to that extent life will be peaceful and calm and the world will seem trustable, bright, and illuminated with glory.

Several Exercises

Observing the Picture-Making Function:
Think through one of your activities. Think about the pictures you create in imagination and see if you can feel how they pull you ahead. What happened that you ended up at the sink instead of the stove? Why did you decide to mow the lawn now? Not the reasons, but what was the picture in your head that got you out the door and how did it pull you? The height of the grass? The shine of the new mower? The bikini-wearing woman sunning next door? Why didn't you stop at the grocery store? What was the picture in your mind? Crowded check-out lines? Or the frozen dinner already in your freezer?

Observing Your Anxiety:
A) Create a list of your fears.
B) See if you can notice your anxiety. If you are not blissfully happy, there is some anxiety blocking your awareness. It might be one of those from the list of fears just above.

Observing the Creative Anxiety Process at Work:
1) Take a breath or two and notice your body, how you are sitting and breathing. Look around to see if there is anything interesting to do. Since this is an experiment, you need not discover anything important, indeed,

perhaps it would be best if it were something small. Raise or lower the shade. Turn the light off or on. Make a cup of coffee.
2) Whatever you decide on, for the sake of this experiment, do not do it immediately. If you do it immediately, you will not experience the cycle. Allow an image to form of you doing whatever you have chosen. See the shade pulled, the light on, the coffee made. When you do anything, this imaging of an agreeable future happens, but usually so quickly you do not notice it happening.
3) Sharpen your focus on that picture until it becomes that which you most want to do in life right now. Observe it until you have a feeling-response of attraction to it. Stare at it until a definite intention to do it forms.
4) Allow yourself to feel the deep pull, the anxiety within you, to get to the job and do something. Since this is a small task, the pull will be small, but it is there. Sit with it for a while.
5) Then act slowly. As a film in slow motion, allow your acting to unreel. The shade moves slowly. The switch unfortunately just clicks, but crossing to it can be slow and deliberate, and observing the change in light can continue with two or three flicks of the switch, but slowly. The coffee making can become a series of imagined images, with each action held in abeyance until the anxiety rises.
6) Continue to observe the anxiety drop as the gap between image and reality closes. Until you are experiencing peace and brightness.

Observing the Pull of Cultural Pictures:

As you move through the rest of today, simply try to be aware of when you are following a cultural picture without thinking or feeling. Just say to yourself:

- This cup of coffee is being drunk because everybody is supposed to need a cup of coffee in the morning, not

because I am thirsty for coffee or feel any chemical draw to it.
- This is not my kind of car, but it fits what a person with my salary should drive.
- I am in church, but I don't enjoy church. I am in church because it is the thing to do.
- I am talking about football because us guys are supposed to like the stupid sport.
- I am answering this question because it would be impolite not to.
- I am working my butt off to be selected for a job I will not enjoy.
- I am desperately trying to get my weight down until I can wear the jeans I wore as a teenager.

Play this game a bit, and you will be surprised at how far you can go in a day without a self-chosen and conscious impulse.

Observing Self-Preserving Pictures:

A) List for yourself ten self-preserving pictures you carry around that impact your behavior. You might want to review them for what should go on the discard list, what on the alter list, and what on the cherish list.

B) List three things you do all the time. Next to each of them, write one small thing you could do that would be different. Rank them in order of difficulty. Do the easiest.

Observing the Here and Now:

From time to time, stop everything and be aware of your internal and external surroundings. The Buddha gives you four categories of things to be aware of: Your body, your feelings, your thoughts, and your surroundings. Then try moving slowly and staying in touch with all that. A thirty-second exercise.

Observing the Passage to Intention:

1) Sit quietly for a moment, focus on your breath; get yourself prepared for observing the experiment.
2) Think of something you could do, and allow yourself to begin to feel and respond to it. Write down a couple of words as a title for it.
   Do nothing.
3) Think of something else you could do, and allow yourself to begin to feel and respond to it. Again, make a note to refer to.
   Do nothing.
4) Think of something else you could do, and allow yourself to begin to feel and respond to it. Make a third note on the page.
   Do nothing.
5) Now begin to review the alternatives simply by allowing your attention to move from one note to another to another.

Until one rises from the others, demanding action. Wait for the intention to settle in and the anxiety to act on the intention to rise.

Do it.

Are you awake? This exercise wakes me up every time.

My Bookshelf

The book you have read is the work of a spiritual teacher functioning as a spiritual teacher does. I have been slow to cite specific authors as sources for specific statements because my task is to seek knowledge from authorities, bring it into my heart, and then replay it as my knowledge. For if it has been truly brought to heart, it is truly my knowledge, and I no longer can safely attribute it to another. Indeed, those others might find it irritating to see their doctrines mixed with other people's ideas, shaken in my heart, and then spilled forth as theirs.

So what I can do for you is give you the books sitting on the top row of my bookshelf, those most relevant to this work. You may well want to read them and allow them into your heart, that you might shake them up and pour them out as your knowledge.

"**" indicates a book at the heart of this discussion.
"*" indicates a book directly relevant to this discussion.
"No asterisk" indicates a book impinging on but not central to this discussion.

** Almaas, A. H. *The Point of Existence*. Berkeley: Diamond Books, 1995.
Arasteh, A. Reza. *Final Integration in the Adult Personality*. Leiden: E. J. Brill, 1965.

Barfield, Owen. *Saving the Appearances*. Hanover: Wesleyan University Press, 1988.
* Becker, Ernest. *The Denial of Death*. New York: Free Press, 1973.
Buber, Martin. *I and Thou*. New York: Simon and Schuster, 1996.
** Burtt, E. A., ed. *The Teachings of the Compassionate Buddha*. New York: Mentor Books, 1982.
* Chardin, Teilhard. *The Future of Man*. New York: Harper and Row, 1964.
** Chardin, Teilhard. *The Phenomenon of Man*. New York: Harper Torchbooks, 1965.
Chetwynd, Tom. *Zen and the Kingdom of Heaven*. Boston: Wisdom Publications, 2001.
** Cowan, John. *Taking Jesus Seriously: Buddhist Meditation for Christians*. Collegeville: Liturgical Press, 2004.
Culligan, Kevin, Mary Jo Meadow, and Daniel Chowning. *Purifying the Heart: Buddhist Meditation for Christians*. New York: Crossroad, 1994.
Dalai Lama. *How to Practice*. New York: Pocket Books, 2002.
* Fleischman, Paul. *Karma and Chaos*. Seattle: Vipassana Research Publication, 1999.
** Gunaratana, Henepola. *Mindfulness in Plain English*. Boston: Wisdom, 1991.
** Hart, William. *Vipassana Meditation as Taught by S.N. Goenka*. New York: Harper and Row, 1991.
** Klein, Jean. *Be Who You Are*. London: Watkins, 1973.
** Klein, Jean. *Who am I?*. Rockport: Element, 1988.
** Brother Lawrence. *The Practice of the Presence of God*. White Plains: Peter Pauper, 1963.
Morinaga, Soko. *Novice to Master*. Boston: Wisdom Publications, 2002.
Rinpoche, Thrangu. *Everyday Consciousness and Buddha Awakening*. New York: Snow Lion Publications, 2002.

** Roberts, Bernadette. *The Experience of No-Self.* Boulder and London: Shambhala, 1984.
* Sinetar, Marsha. *Ordinary People as Monks and Mystics.* New York: Paulist Press, 1986.
* Suzuki, D. T. *The Awakening of Zen.* Boston and London: Shambhala, 2000.
* Suzuki, D. T. *Introduction to Zen Buddhism.* New York: Grove, 1964.
Suzuki, D. T., Erich Fromm, and Richard DeMartino. *Zen Buddhism and Psychoanalysis.* New York: Grove, 1963.
* Suzuki, Shunryu. *Zen Mind, Beginner's Mind.* New York: Weatherhill, 2000.
** Thera, Nyanaponika. *The Heart of Buddhist Meditation.* York Beach: Samuel Weiser, 1965.
** Tolle, Eckhart. *A New Earth*, New York: Penguin, 2006.
** Tolle, Eckhart. *The Power of Now.* Novato: New World Library, 1999.
* Watts, Alan. *The Art of Contemplation.* New York: Pantheon, 1972.
Watts, Alan. *Tao: The Watercourse Way.* New York: Pantheon, 1975.
* Wegner, Michael, ed. *Wind Bell.* Berkeley: North Atlantic Books, 2002.
* Whitehead, Alfred. *Process and Reality.* New York: The Free Press, 1978.
Wilber, Ken. *The Marriage of Sense and Soul.* New York Broadway Books, 1999.
* Wilber, Ken. *No Boundary.* Boston and London: Shambhala, 1985.

About the Author

At age seventy-three, John Cowan has retired from all pursuits other than riding a motorcycle and teaching meditation. Unlike most authors of books on meditation who write as if meditation is all they have done with their lives, in writing this book he draws on his experiences as a laborer, union member, monastic seminarian, Roman Catholic priest, husband and father, corporate manager, athlete, sailor, Episcopal priest, student of Zen, *vipassana* meditator, consultant to business, nonprofits, and government, and of course, teacher of meditation, long-distance motorcycle rider and camper, and Quaker. He is the author of four published books: *The Self-Reliant Manager* (AMACOM, 1977), *Small Decencies* (HarperBusiness, 1992), *The Common Table* (HarperBusiness, 1993), and *Taking Jesus Seriously: Buddhist Meditation for Christians* (Liturgical Press, 2004).

His wife is Edith Meissner, who is her own woman. His sons are Benjamin and David, both a vast improvement on himself. His daughters-in-law are Megan and Sarah, for whom he has both respect and feelings of tenderness. About the time this book is printed, the first grandchild should have arrived, and the second is following in four months. That fills him with delight.